On the Road to V
The Flexible Future of

Published by Viction:ary
Edited & Designed by TwoPoints.Net

"To mention both typographic, and, in the same breath/
sentence, grids, is strictly tautologous."
Anthony Froshaug (The Designer, no. 167, January 1967)

Years may have passed since the statement above was made, but the same can still
be said about variable typography today. Typography is already a highly variable
system in itself, spanning the architecture of a single letter right up to the composition of a body of text. As such, combining the words "variable" and "typography" can
be seen as repetitive.

More than 500 years ago, Gutenberg[1] adapted movable type printing to
the western languages. The justified text in his masterpiece, the 42-line Bible,
is still superior in quality to many of the others we are able to produce with our
contemporary design tools, and he achieved this simply by using multiple versions of each letter with different widths. Frank Blokland[2], founder of the Dutch
Type Library, observed that Gutenberg probably chose a modular calligraphic
font, Textura, as the model for his movable type to be able to calculate these differences – and he was probably right. If the number of letters and their amount of
units can be determined, one can easily calculate and adjust the number of units
used accordingly.

A modular approach to create a variable typographic system can be found
as well in Josef Albers'[3] typeface, Kombinationsschrift, from 1930. Albers' system
allowed the typeface to change not only in width, but also in height and weight. This
definition of variability made sense for Kombinationsschrift, as it was supposed to
be used as a display typeface and not for longer texts. There are plenty more exam-
ples in history that show variability as an inherent attribute to typography.

Why emphasise on the variable aspect of typography now?

On 14 September 2016, Adobe, Google, Apple, and Microsoft announced a new
update to the OpenType specification to introduce variable fonts. Similar to the
multiple master concept, it will allow for custom styles to be generated from a single font file, so that designers have a tool that lets them choose any weight between
two extremes. What we at TwoPoints.Net personally find most exciting is that
these fonts will be made responsive on websites. This means that they will be able
to automatically adjust to the size and aspect ratio of the viewport.

Since this update, almost everybody in the type world has been talking
about variable fonts. While the technology has yet to be fully implemented and
critical voices deem it to be a trend until it can be applied practically, variable
typography in a broader sense is already an unstoppable force in contemporary
communication design. To us, variable typography is not just about variable fonts,

1   Johannes Gensfleisch zur Laden zum Gutenberg was born in 1400 in Mainz, Germany. He was
a blacksmith, goldsmith, printer, and publisher. He is famously known for introducing mechanical movable type printing to Europe, with which he printed his major work, the 42-line Bible.

2   Frank E. Blokland was born in 1959 in Leiden, the Netherlands. Founder of the Dutch Type
Library, he has been teaching at the Royal Academy of Arts in The Hague since 1987, and the
Plantin Institute of Typography in Antwerp since 1995. Blokland defended his PhD disserta-
tion, *On the Origin of Patterning in Movable Latin Type: Renaissance Standardisation, Systematisation,
and Unitisation of Textura and Roman Type* in 2016 at the University of Leiden. His research was
conducted to test the hypothesis that Gutenberg developed a standardised and unified system
for the production of Textura type.

3   Josef Albers was born in 1888 in Bottrop, Germany. He was a student and teacher at the Bauhaus,
as well as an internationally renowned artist. Apart from his paintings, Albers' best known lega-
cy is the book, *The Interaction of Colors*.

but also about the evolution from static to flexible in almost all aspects of communication design, if not design in general. In fact, we have been witnessing this change for quite some time now in the fields of generative design, liquid/fluid/dynamic visual identities, evolutive/living visual systems, and kinetic/responsive typography, where there are as many experiments as there are terms to describe them.

An experiment's viability depends on its applicability, but in this case, not all of them are true experiments. What they all have in common is the ability to adapt to fast-changing contexts, both semiological and morphological. Responsive websites have become the new standard, because our communication behaviour is rooted in our multiple screen use. While visual diversity meant additional costs in the times of print-dominated communication, multiple images on multiple formats as well as moving images are the norm in screen-based communication today. Unresponsive websites that result in illegibility have been penalised by Google since 2015 with lower rankings on Google Search. In 2018, Google even announced that mobile-friendly sites would be indexed before desktop-friendly sites.

Only the future will tell how successful variable typography will become. Even though type designers are still experimenting with new technology and only some browsers and software support it, it seems to have hit the nerve of our time in a general sense. With that in mind, this book aims to provide a glimpse into its excitingly eclectic world.

How is this book meant to be read?

We initially structured the contents of this book around traditional typographic weights, but in the course of putting them together, we quickly realised that

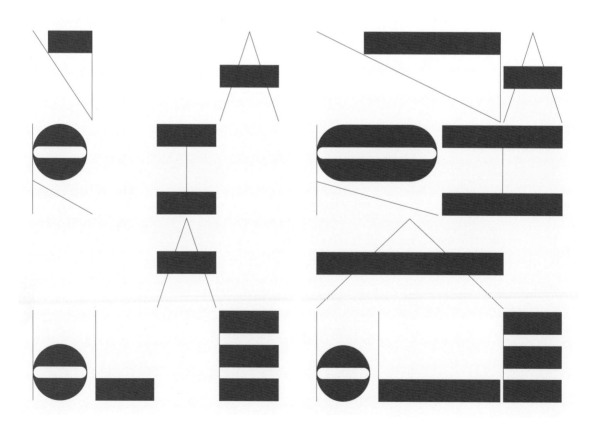

Variable *Position*   Variable *Position, Width*

the light/bold (thin/thick), condensed/extended (narrow/wide), and regular/italic (upright/slanted) ranges were not the only extremes possible, and anything in-between could be interpolated. As such, we ended up re-evaluating and re-organising the work we received from all the featured design studios into the following sections:

In variable typography, we are typically able to see a sequence of events – a before and an after. For example, visiting a responsive website on a mobile device and then a desktop makes the rules of variability become clear through comparison. With kinetic typography, it becomes even more obvious, as we are forced to follow an animation frame by frame to understand the font's variability.

On the other hand, a book can be read both in sequence or as a single image if one were to be looking at a double-page spread as a whole. As readers, we get to decide how to flip the pages and how to move our eyes over each page, whether we start from the beginning to the end or from the end to the beginning. We can even speed it up or slow it down to create so-called "animations" at our own pace.

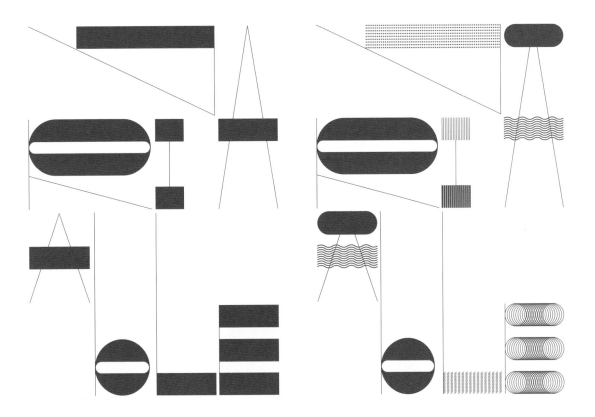

Variable *Position, Width, Height*   Variable *Position, Width, Height, Styles*

How did this book idea come about?

The book you are holding in your hands has evolved many times, and while this may not be unusual when it comes to publishing, the reasons behind its changes shed an interesting light on the subject matter at hand. In sharing them, we first need to go back to 2009, when the idea for *I Love Type (ILT)* was born.

ILT was a series we developed with viction:ary to honour famous typefaces like *Futura, Avant Garde, Bodoni, DIN, Gill Sans, Franklin Gothic, Helvetica*, and *Times*. It was created out of our interest to explore how classic typefaces were being used in contemporary graphic design at the time. As students in the late 1990s, we were taught to stick to the "all-time classics" in order to become good typographers. As we became teachers ourselves later on, we began to understand the benefit of limiting typeface choices for the untrained eye, and saw a deeper reason for it than just to limit potential "damage". It was a credible design approach, in that using an often-seen, less expressive typeface actually gave one more freedom and room for creativity because the audience's eye would not be instantly drawn to the typeface itself, but rather, to what was done *with* the typeface or the space around it.

When we published *ILT*, many design studios had been working with the same typefaces for decades. Even though these typefaces were typically attached to specific time periods, the ways with which they were treated to look contemporary surprised and excited us. As such, it was important for us to introduce the typefaces' histories at the beginning of each book before revealing the creative work to evoke the same emotions in readers.

The series had to come to an end after eight volumes, not just because we had finished covering the most popular typefaces out there, but also due to the fact that designers everywhere had begun changing their approach to typography. Instead of sticking to the all-time classics, they started becoming more experimental by using and making new typefaces. Distinctiveness began to rule over perfection, and instead of perceiving it as a negative development, we saw it open up a whole new playground in the design world. Typography has never been as flexible as it is today, and we are proud to have made a book on a subject matter that deserves to be delved into, no matter how many changes it goes through.

Martin Lorenz, Ph.D.
TwoPoints.Net

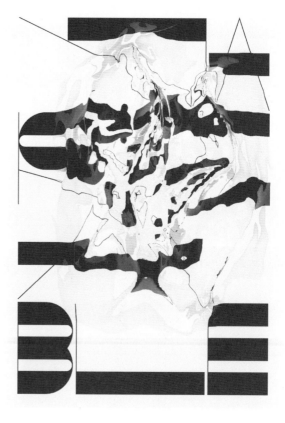

Variable *through transformation*. Transformation of the letters through the tools that have been used to draw them (Calligraphy, Lettering) or the distortion of the letters by process (Filter) or perspective (Object (Glass, Fabric)).

Studio Feixen
Interview

With Felix Pfäffli *by* Martin Lorenz

Studio Feixen is an independent Design Studio based in Lucerne, Switzerland. They work globally with clients like Nike, Google, Hermès, and The New York Times, as well as locally with institutions like the Wanderlust, the Nuits Sonores Festival, the Lucerne University of Applied Sciences and Arts, Südpol, and the Luzerner Theatre.

Martin Lorenz spoke with Felix Pfäffli, who founded Studio Feixen in 2009. Felix teaches at the Fachklasse Grafik Luzern, and is the youngest member in the history of AGI. Besides winning prizes worldwide, he has also given lectures and organised exhibitions and workshops. In his own words, he is responsible for the "necessary chaos" in Studio Feixen's designs.

M.L.:We see a trend in design that is moving from static solutions towards flexible systems. The term "variable typography", as it is used in this book, tries to embrace all aspects of design which have made typography more flexible in the recent years, whether they are in the form of flexible visual identities, moving posters, or variable fonts. Amid all this, Studio Feixen has became one of the spearheads in the "moving posters" movement. Could you tell us a little bit about your studio?

F.P.: Studio Feixen is just Raphael Leutenegger and I, Felix Pfäffli, but we usually work in a group of four. We are a graphic design studio at our core, but like to believe that we have no clear boundaries as to which fields we work in. We are much more interested in creating our lives, rather than creating work. We work on commercial projects four days a week, but reserve one day a week to work for ourselves. On this day, which is usually Friday, we experiment with stuff that we want to do in the future.

ML: What are you experimenting with at the moment?
FP: We do all kinds of stuff. We experiment with fonts, of course. We created a font that allows us to design faster; one that is made to stretch, because we needed a digital tool that could sort of match the speed of sketching on a paper. We are also working on our own line of clothing, and opening a restaurant very soon. It is going to be a pizzeria. (Laughs) On top of that, we are working on an exhibition made of cakes, which is soon to be seen in China. Maybe we will even start an object series with plexiglass in the near future. So you see, it is a colourful mix of stuff. The ideas often appear during the week, and we then work on them on Fridays.

ML: Interesting! Did you have any specific motive in taking Fridays off to work on self-commissioned projects, or have you always been working like this?

1　The Wanderlust is a cultural establishment in the centre of Paris. Besides housing a restaurant, a music club, an open-air cinema, and a bar, it also offers a variety of activities like morning yoga training. For its reopening in the summer of 2014, we developed a playful and colourful design concept that we propagated through illegal and, for a time, anonymous placards throughout Paris. The posters featured bright patterns, smiles, and arrows pointing in all directions; making it seem as though we were playing Tetris with them. Beyond the venue itself, we applied our designs throughout the city and across all other applications. To simplify the latter process, we developed a flexible font family so that we did not have to design one poster after another from then on, and simply let the computer generate them for us.

FP: We have always worked like this. Every half a year, we question our way of working. When you create your own company, you are also responsible for everyone working within the company. What we try to do is create a space that makes us happy every day. Since the beginning, it was clear to us that we needed a space to work without any boundaries. Of course, we are very lucky with our clients. We can do almost whatever we want, but still, there are boundaries in every project. During our free time, we really can do anything. We believe that if you do not take time for yourself, you will be always stuck with what your clients want from you – which is why we want to be in control over our future. Our future clients do not know what we have in our heads and what we want to do later on, so we have to show them.

ML: The very first time I became aware of Studio Feixen was in 2014 through your posters for Süd-pol. There was already a strong focus on variable typography, even though they were not animated. It was not until 2017 that I came to know about your "moving posters". It almost seemed like a reinvention of your studio's focus. What happened in between 2014 and 2017?

FP: (Laughs) For Südpol, there was simply no time to animate the posters even though I had been doing "moving posters" from before, as seen in my final graduation project in 2010 about randomness. When Raphael joined the studio, we decided to become the kind of studio that always looked for new solutions, and it became logical for us to move in the direction of "moving posters". Since then, almost every project we have done is flexible, animated, and responsive. Time itself is an important variable in our work, and I guess it all started with the Wanderlust[1] posters. This project was really flexible in nature. Every element was designed to adjust responsively without ever becoming boring. The application of the corporate design was actually fun, because you could play with the individual elements like Lego and be surprised with every new outcome.

I

ML: Does time as a variable convert a visual identity into an evolving one?

FP: It is a pity that this is not apparent from our website, but if you could have taken a closer look at the Wanderlust's smiley face poster in real life, you would have been able to see that the dots started off very large in size. Our idea was for them to shrink with every passing year to transform the pattern and subsequently, the visual identity as a whole; making the latter less strict and more open. To use time as variable, it really depends if you can design an evo-lutive visual identity for a project or not. If you are hired to design a visual identity for only one event, then you cannot really develop a story.

ML: Agreed. Through application, it is easy to see the flexibility of a visual identity, but even if you do not see it, it does not mean that the visual identity you designed is not flexible or even evolutive.

FP: Absolutely! Take our work for "20 Minuten"[2], the biggest newspaper in Switzerland, for example. When designing a newspaper, you design for all possible variations and, to me, this is why I think a newspaper is already animated in nature. Nothing is static. Some days, the headline could be very long, resulting in smaller images, and vice versa. All the elements are reacting to each other. In line with this, everything we do nowadays is flexible, and the systems we create are always made to react to every new situation.

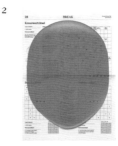

2

ML: Although motion design has become more acces-sible for graphic designers over the last decade, do you think it is still not common for graphic design-ers to know how to animate, especially those among the older generation?

FP: Yes, that is absolutely true. However, through the newspaper project, I found that even though the older generation does not usually think by way of animation, they do understand flexible systems. The main difference between them and the gener-ation today lies in the way that we make the flexi-bility visible through our websites. In our Shorties[3] project, the animations showed all the possibilities each system had, and every single frame could have become a poster by itself. They showed our audiences what we did, and could have done.

2   We had the pleasure of completely redesigning "20 Minuten", the most widely read newspaper in Switzerland, as part of a campaign for Samsung. In collaboration with Jung von Matt, we designed a newspaper that was – for once – intended more to be looked at, than read. To achieve this feat, we first redesigned the entire layout without losing all of its nuances, such as the visuals of the horoscopes, the logos of the television stations, a tragically-odd comic, as well as an "emotional" weather map. On a second layer, each page was confronted with a colourful interpretation of its content. While we had to squeeze several months of hard labour into a few weeks of hard development work, we succeeded in making not only the design edition itself unique, but also every single page within stand out.

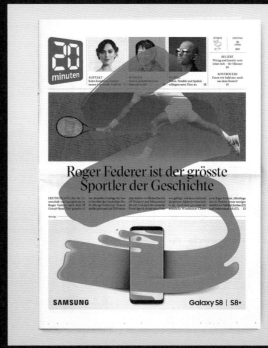

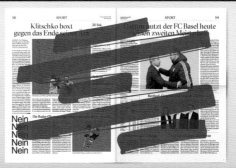

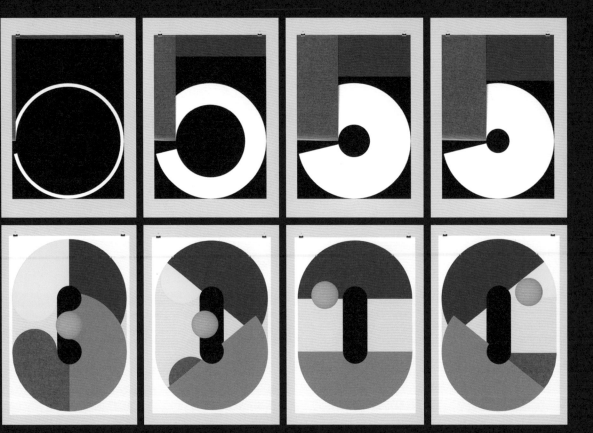

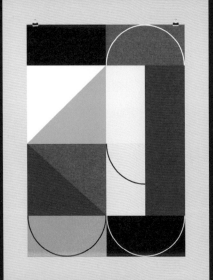

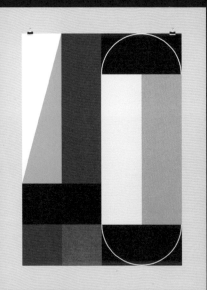

3   Over time, we have developed
    the habit of translating the
    happenings in our studio into
    animations for the Insta world.
    Whether we simply discovered
    a new caffeine-boosting drink in
    the beverages isle, or suddenly
    developed an interest in the
    space between animation and
    typography, for whatever reason,
    we do not want to reserve our
    findings from you.

3

ML: How has your work evolved over the years?

FP: We want to learn something new with every project, and each one should be a step forward. The longer I work in this profession, the more connected everything feels. When I started my career, designing a poster felt like a challenge. After designing my first book, the first visual identity and so forth, I then began to gain a broader understanding of the possibilities offered by each of these applications. The more knowledge you gain, the more flexible you become; allowing you to combine the applications in the weirdest ways and bring out each of their strengths best. At Studio Feixen, we are continuously searching for surprising ways to design applications so it never becomes repetitive, and things just keep getting more and more interesting with each project. Take our Oto Nové Swiss[4] project for example. Although the creative outcome looked like a poster, it was actually not one per se because it was never printed. The only place where it was displayed was on their website.

4

ML: Do you think variable typography is a natural evolution from static typography as digital devices have become widespread?

FP: Yes, absolutely. I think it is a natural evolution. Everytime a new technology appears, everybody starts experimenting with it. When you see everything becoming responsive and you happen to be into typography, you would probably start experimenting with responsive typography. If you are into images, you will experiment with images.
I saw this new technology the other day that makes images responsive, where they do not just simply stretch, but re-invent themselves at the same time. Everybody is experimenting with flexibility on all levels right now.

ML: What do you think is the major advantage of variable typography?

FP: There is a simple reason why typography is becoming more and more important nowadays. Everybody has a smartphone and we are consuming more videos on it, but without sound. This means that we need subtitles to understand what the videos are about. You can already see that subtitles are becoming really important, and designers have started playing around with them. I think there will be a huge step forward in this whole field within the next couple of years because everybody needs subtitles. The typography will be influenced by the image, and the image will be influenced by the typography.

ML: Besides animating typography, your studio creates interactive pieces too. How often do you code?

FP: Once a year, we get involved in a coded project. We do not code a lot because it is not our favourite thing to do. It makes me angry and I think it makes Raphael angry too! (Laughs) Unfortunately sometimes, it is necessary to code – not because we have to, but out of interest. We just wait for the right project to come along. Coding is nothing we can delegate. We need to do it ourselves. While coding, you get to learn so many things that you might be able to use in another project. We would lose a lot of knowledge if we hired a coder, as we would be stuck and unable to develop an original idea any further.

ML: Working with code makes you rethink your original ideas. Does that mean that code is not just the realisation of an idea, but a language to question the idea and further develop it?

FP: Coding is like thinking to us. For projects like "20 Minuten", the process of development is like coding for us. If the headline grows longer, the image becomes smaller. The entire length of text might even increase, causing the text at the bottom to be lost. It is all connected. When we talk about our work in the studio, we mostly talk about the capabilities of each of element. What can this element do? Can it run around the format? Can it appear here and then there? Design is about the behaviour of elements. A coder thinks in the exact same way.

ML: Even if you do not write code, do you design as if you were coding?

FP: Absolutely. When you are hired for a corporate design project, you are hired to make rules. Even though we do not like making rules, it is our task to make them.

ML: Can you describe your design process?

FP: That really depends on the project. Every project leads to a different process. When we have to be really professional, we spend a lot of time sketching out the system, until it is flawless. The system is the most important part of the project, as it needs to be able to process all the information. If we work on a project that needs to be animated later, we work first on a storyboard, sketch every possible moment of the animation, and then produce the animation. We do this so that nothing can go wrong. I enjoy the process most when the design transforms constantly. Having the whole studio working on a project can take it in any direction at any time, but we have one simple rule: we never go back. We love to make decisions. If we have said "no" to a direction, we never revisit it, but it is always possible to spin it into a new direction. If we have a new idea that changes the original idea a lot and is better than the original direction, we explore the new direction. We have projects that I absolutely love which are changing all the time. They are often the most time-consuming to work on, but turn out the nicest because you are not committed to one idea, but the best possible outcome. As a designer, this means that you also need to be super flexible, and cannot fall in love with an idea. You need to go with what is best.

ML: How do you decide what is best? What is your criteria?

FP: The gut. (Laughs) No, we discuss the ideas. We have another rule. We actually have a lot of rules! When you talk about abandoning an idea and you see that someone in the group is sad about losing it, then most of the time, this person is right. When you are sad about losing an idea, it means that you see something in this idea that the rest of the group has not seen. We decide then to work on it for a couple more hours to make it visible.

ML: How do you think the way we learn, teach and design will change with design becoming more flexible?

FP: I think it will change a lot. The way I teach today is really different to the way I was taught. Today, you educate individuals even though you have absolutely no clue what their future will be like. The professions are changing in an incredible rapid way, and you cannot be sure that what you are teaching your students will end up being exercised later on. That is why, what you need to teach is flexibility. I find that a big problem is the sense of individuality. Students have to learn how to work together, but a lot are working against each other.

ML: So, you are teaching teamwork?

FP: Yes. I do a lot of different subjects. One of my favourite subjects is called "Generative Design". It is based on the idea of Conditional Design[5] by Studio Moniker. The members of Studio Moniker meet every Tuesday to work together as if they are a programme. I began doing the same with Tobias Hauser, the dean of the school I am teaching at. The students have to design programmes, but they are also part of the programme. They can do whatever they want, but they have to present their results at the end. They learn a lot through this project because they have to organise their materials, discuss how to work together, and more. While they are being trained in all the skills they need to be a graphic designer this way, they do not really realise it because they are so busy all the time. The next step is then to make a real visual identity. The students love this. It is a mixture of fun and super hard work.

ML: Why do you think this differs to the way you were taught before?

FP: I think this is more pedagogic. We are talking much more about education and how to educate today than before. The generations before us were often famous designers, who were mostly interested in their own careers and taught a certain way. Today, I think the fame of a single designer is less important. For me, it is much more interesting to see a student finding his own language than copying mine. It makes more sense. I get the feeling that we are closer to the students today than before. Before, there was a bigger distance between student and teacher.

ML: Does it mean that you do not believe in the future of the individual star designer, but in the designer as a part of a collaborative effort, changing according to context?

FP: Yes. Absolutely. At our school, we are very active at the moment to change that. It is amazing to see how much change is possible. The mixture is very interesting. You have old and young teachers, and they are all interested in new ways of teaching.

ML: Felix, thank you so much!

FP: My pleasure.

<hr>

5   Conditional Design is a design method formulated by Studio Moniker graphic designers Luna Maurer, Jonathan Puckey, Roel Wouters, and the artist Edo Paulus, which foregrounds process over finished products. As a design strategy, it is defined by playfully designed sets of rules and conditions that stimulate collaboration between participants and lead to unpredictable outcomes. Visit workbook. conditionaldesign.org for more information.

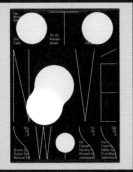
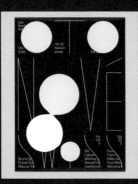
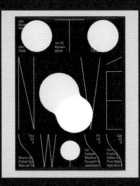
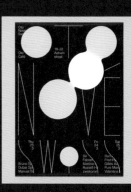

4 Oto Nové Swiss is a three-day festival at London's Cafe Oto. One year, we were asked to design whatever we thought suited the event best. Since the festival was organised by Swiss cultural institutes but based in London, we thought that it did not make sense to advertise it on the streets. As such, we decided to design an interactive poster that viewers could explore, play around with, and perhaps even compose their own music with. Visit otonoveswiss.co.uk for the full experience, and if you happen to be in London during the festival period, do not miss it and say "hi" to all of our friends from Switzerland!

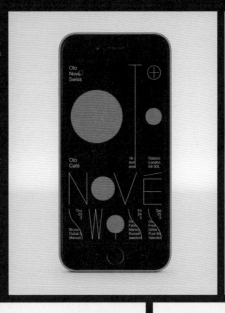
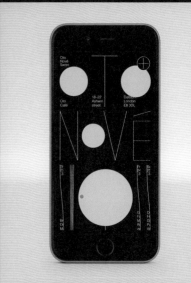

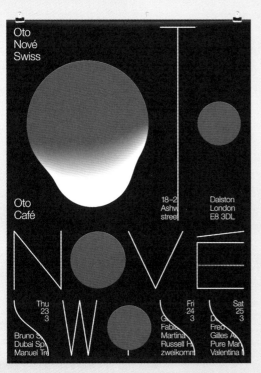
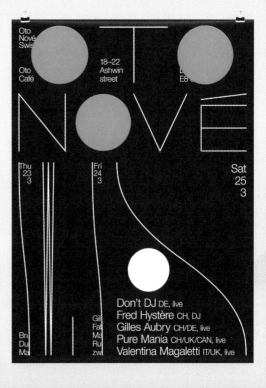

Dia
Interview

With Mitch Paone *by* Martin Lorenz

DIA is a Brooklyn-based creative studio specialising in kinetic identity systems, graphic design, and typography. The core team are Mitch Paone, Meg Donohoe, and Deanna Sperrazza. With clients ranging from Nike and Samsung to the U.N., DIA's work has reached international fame through the their unique mixture of traditional and kinetic typography. Martin Lorenz spoke with Mitch Paone, the founder and creative director of DIA.

M.L.:Before we dive into the subject of variable typography, could you share a little bit about your background? What did you do before founding DIA with Meg Donohoe?

M.P.: I studied Graphic Design and Jazz Performance at the Loyola University of New Orleans until 2005, which is probably a better school for music than for design. After leaving the university, I almost immediately started freelancing in the field of motion graphics. I went to Los Angeles and worked for a large list of motion design companies, among them Logan, Brand New School, and Psyop. Until 2009, I was working mainly in film titles, commercial directing, animation, and motion design, but then I made a transition towards advertisement. I had to figure out what the heck I wanted to do, and this is when I met Meg, who is my wife and business partner now. We met freelancing at a motion graphics company in New York. While working at this company, we saw that there was a huge range of work that could be done in the field of motion graphics, which made us found DIA. In the beginning, DIA really was a motion graphics company. We were working mostly for advertising agencies doing commercials from 2009 up until 2013, when we had another transition towards a more traditional design practice.

ML: How many people work at DIA?

MP: We are four at the moment: Meg, me, Daniel (Wenzel), and Deanna (Sperrazza) who has been with us for almost four years now. Sometimes we have interns, but not too often. Daniel is an exception. He was very persistent. (Laughs) Joking aside, he was a good fit and we had project inflow. We thought he could be really helpful with the incoming projects and we could teach him a couple of things too. We usually do not bring in additional designers. Most of the design work is handled by Deanna and myself. Meg operates the business and provides really helpful feedback and direction from a non-designer's perspective. DIA has been bigger, but three or four as a core team is where we want to keep things. We do not see any reason to expand at the moment.

ML: What is your work process like?

MP: The way we work is very share-oriented. Everybody works on every project. I usually initiate creative direction, but this does not mean that I am the only one who can propose ideas. We have a very iterative way of working. We try to do as much stuff as possible in a very short period of time by just throwing it out there and seeing what sticks. Then, we usually discuss the directions and decide which one feels worth developing further. Everything feels very open. In a specific realm, Daniel is much better in coding than I am, so I handle more of the animation side of things and he handles more of the scripting stuff. Deanna is really good at front-end development and digital design applications, so if we have a concept, we essentially parcel it out to where each other's strengths lie. I also usually oversee the consistency of all deliverables, and that the typesetting is done well. I am probably the most hardcore of us three at typesetting stuff. Usually, everything is cool except the typesetting. (Laughs)

ML: The collaborative approach seems to make it difficult to outsource work.

MP: Yes, and that is kind of interesting. When we were a motion graphics company, we were used to outsourcing a lot of work. We were always bringing in animators or illustrators to do a specific task, but I think from a creative development standpoint, the core creativity has to happen internally. It can be really confusing to bring someone in for creative exploration. We can only outsource work when we know exactly what we need, but then, outsourcing is also a way to handle larger projects. While we have animators, type designers, and developers that are able to help out, we have to know exactly what their task will be, otherwise it is going to be a waste of time, effort, and money.

ML: You mentioned your background in Jazz. How does your knowledge about music influence your work as a designer?

MP: Music is probably the most important influence for me. It is difficult to explain this to designers who are not composers, but the way our creative process is set up, models what I do when I compose. While a traditional designer is mostly concerned with the final output, a musician focuses on the process. He works on the vocabulary of the underlying craft. The mastery of that vocabulary allows him to have a conversation, using an instrument. Music provides me with a specific structure, like chord progressions, rhythm, tempo, groove or beat, which I use as my foundation before I decide how I want to work on harmonic structures and instrumentation. If I have a specific looping chord progression that serves as an underlying system, I can be very creative on top of that. That is exactly how we work when we do kinetic typography or motion design. It all goes back to rhythmic looping, pretty much like a chord progression. Music and design are the same to me. One works with sound and the other, with visuals.

ML: Would you say that there are two phases in your creative process when developing variable design? A phase in which you define or create the tools and a phase in which you play with the tools?

MP: Yes, and this is where things get really interesting! Miles Davis is a good example. He experimented with new technologies to create a wider range of expression. Playing with new instruments made him create totally new sounds. The same is happening right now in graphic design with generative design tools. There is an urge to adjust existing tools once we hit a barrier. We modify existing design programmes or create new ones (with processing or openFrameworks) to do a specific task we were not able to do before.

Our background in visual effects has a huge influence on the work we do today. It is a luxury to have knowledge in 3D, visual effects, tracking, and compositing, which were traditionally only used for film. No one really thought about what would happen if we used these tools for graphic design. We always ask ourselves how we can use them in a way they were not intended to be used. Bringing together our knowledge from design and film has generated a lot of the work we did recently. Combining these two worlds gave us results we did not expect. They motivated us to keep on asking ourselves what else we can do.

ML: Kinetic typography has been around for quite a while in cinema and television. It is only in graphic design that it feels like it just arrived. Do you think that this feeling is just a matter of perception or is there really something new happening here? If so, what is it?

MP: I agree that it is a micro-awakening. Kinetic typography has been here before. Take the work by Saul Bass for example. The work he did back in the 1960s is essentially the same as the work we do now. The difference lies in the fact that the output of his work was specific to the content. Design for film has a specific aesthetic. It is completely unrelated to classic editorial design or branding.

1

Another difference is the linear storytelling of kinetic typography for film. You have to watch the whole sequence to understand the story, while in graphic design, we are trying to generate an immediate impression. This is an interesting problem, and where we have done a lot of experiments by asking ourselves how we could take the classic view on design and merge it with the knowledge we have in animation. With the "A-Trak"[1] project, we were pushed to explore these limits. The pressure of the deadline forced us to work fast and with high energy; resulting in the discovery of animating things with no beginning or end. You can render any second of the animation, and it would work as a poster. The design system is built intrinsically into the animation – and this clicked for us at the time. To me, it was the new thing. It was just about connecting the dots. It had been existing, but it never really came together. A book designer would

A-Trak. We have been collaborating with Alain Macklovitch, the DJ and record producer known as A-Trak, since early 2016. We first created a typographic identity system as the foundation for all design. We were then able to create a range of unique artwork for his varying assets working within a set of typographic driven parameters, from the more minimal expression of the brand seen in the website and tour flyers to a maximal expression illustrated in album covers and live show visuals. Special thanks to Evan Brightfield for the Lollapalooza video.

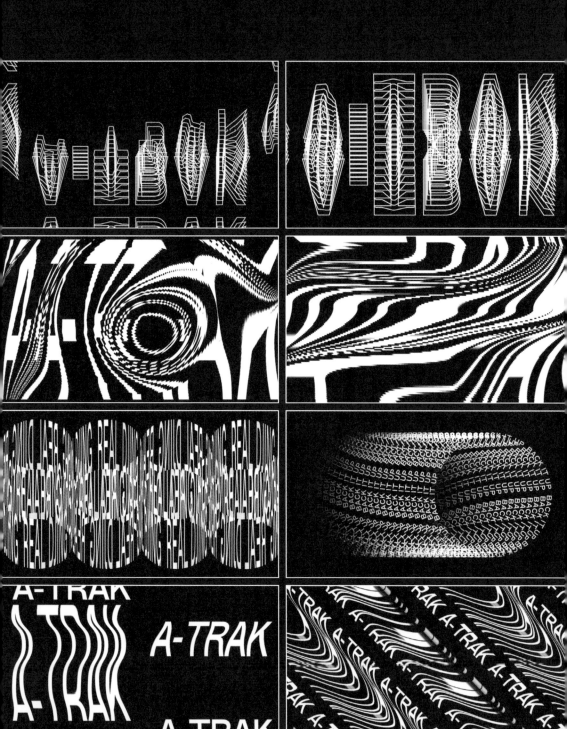

1 A-Trak "In The Loop": A Decade of Remixes is available digitally, on CD, and as a limited edition 7" vinyl box set with custom artwork and a 32-page booklet written by A-Trak. We designed each element from the 12 conceptual typographic covers to the labels for the 45s. We approached each single cover as an individual piece of typographic art thinking about how they could both move and live in print. The goal of each cover was to embody both the music and relate conceptually to the track title. Secondly, we created a minimal typographic identity for the booklet and packaging to support the intensity of the individual artwork. To give the layouts an added conceptual layer, we brought in a looping motif that is pulled from the front and back cover of the box and repeated throughout the spreads and the record labels.

never have thought about this. Similarly, a motion designer would not have thought about designing a book. They are really opposing poles in the design spectrum, but they are coming together now.

ML: In your animated type specimens for Ludovic Balland's typeface, NEXT, you made it look variable even though it actually is not. Where do you see the future for variable fonts?

MP: As much as we do embrace new things, I am very critical about variable fonts. This new technology will only become interesting when it gives us new ways of expression. I think we achieved some interesting solutions[2] playing with the typeface by Ludovic. Animating the different weights of the typeface allowed us to create gradients and patterns, giving us new possibilities for design systems.

2

Variable fonts can be made responsive too. You can make it respond to different behaviours, make it interactive, animate it and, of course, select any weight you like, which is interesting. However, from a practical standpoint, variable fonts are not really exciting to me. One strong typeface and maybe a few extra weights are still enough for most of the design projects. I do not think that this will change anytime soon. Variable fonts are not going to replace a well-drawn small family.

That said, I do think variable fonts are interesting for type designers, as they can be used to build a family really fast. The process of designing a typeface speeds up. In designing typefaces myself, I can generate a large family just by interpolating the steps in between the extremes. This is really helpful. It also helps me to select the right weights. That is actually quite important and interesting.

ML: Many designers were introduced to your work through your typographic experiments, which appear to be in augmented reality. On my end, what amazed me the most was the high quality on all the different levels. The typography and animation are exciting, and they are intrinsically integrated in spaces where we have not seen animated, three-dimensional typography before. Looking at these experiments, it feels like we are getting a glimpse of the future.

MP: (Laughs) Those experiments were actually kind of funny. A lot of them are just prototypes, made with visual effects and not true augmented reality. Only the stuff we do with Zach Lieberman[3] are in true augmented reality. I guess there were moments when I asked myself: could this be viable or not? (Laughs) These experiments kind of freaked me out because they could be the future of how market contents are going to dominate our public spaces. There is no way that the visualisation will be tasteful typography. They will be ads. This freaked me out a little bit, but you cannot stop where things are going – it will happen. In the future, phones will likely have augmented reality integrated into their software and it will no longer be necessary for us to download an app for it anymore. However, until augmented reality is integrated in our devices, these experiments are not going to be used for anything else than just fun projects.

I am also relatively critical about the level of interaction people care about. I noticed this in our design projects. There is always an interactive experience that people get excited about, but all in all, people like passive experiences and already get excited about seeing something moving. If it requires too much work, then the engagement tends to develop not much further. Like flash websites back in the day. People were like, "yeah, I do not have the patience for this". There is a nice middle-ground that could possibly happen. I think this is why our augmented reality experiments worked. You get enough of that passive experience. Kinetic type animations applied to space, even without real augmented reality, could be extremely powerful and visually captivating, but I still think that we are in a realm of technical barriers to be able to pull this off. Even if we could do that in true augmented reality, we would not be able to get the perfect composited and tracked animation we are getting now because the result would be a little bit janky and weird.

From a learning standpoint I find these experiments extremely interesting. To be able to deal with text in an environmental context, that really has no format and no boundaries, is a problem that designers never really had to deal with before. Our typographic history is influenced by specific formats. The Swiss have a huge body of visual research done about how to design a poster, but all the posters have the exact same format. In the United States, we do not have fixed formats. We always have to think about flexibility in our work because it is never going to be applied to only one format. Augmented reality is going to be a whole new ball game, having no formats at all. For example: how do you deal with exhibition content? Do

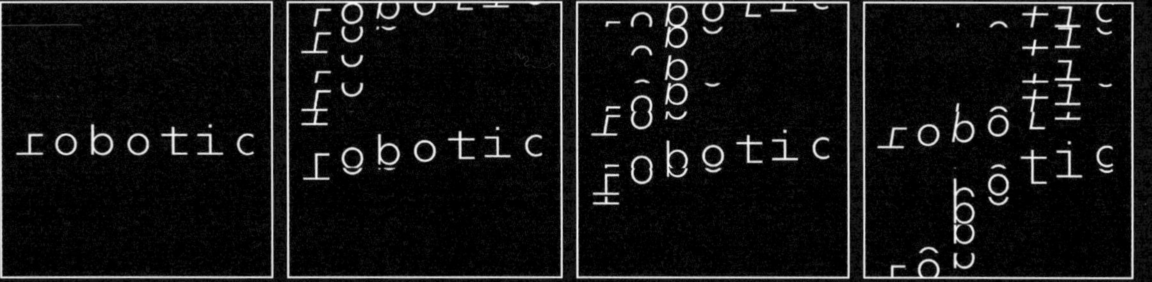

2 Kinetic typographic specimens for
   Next Typeface by Ludovic Balland

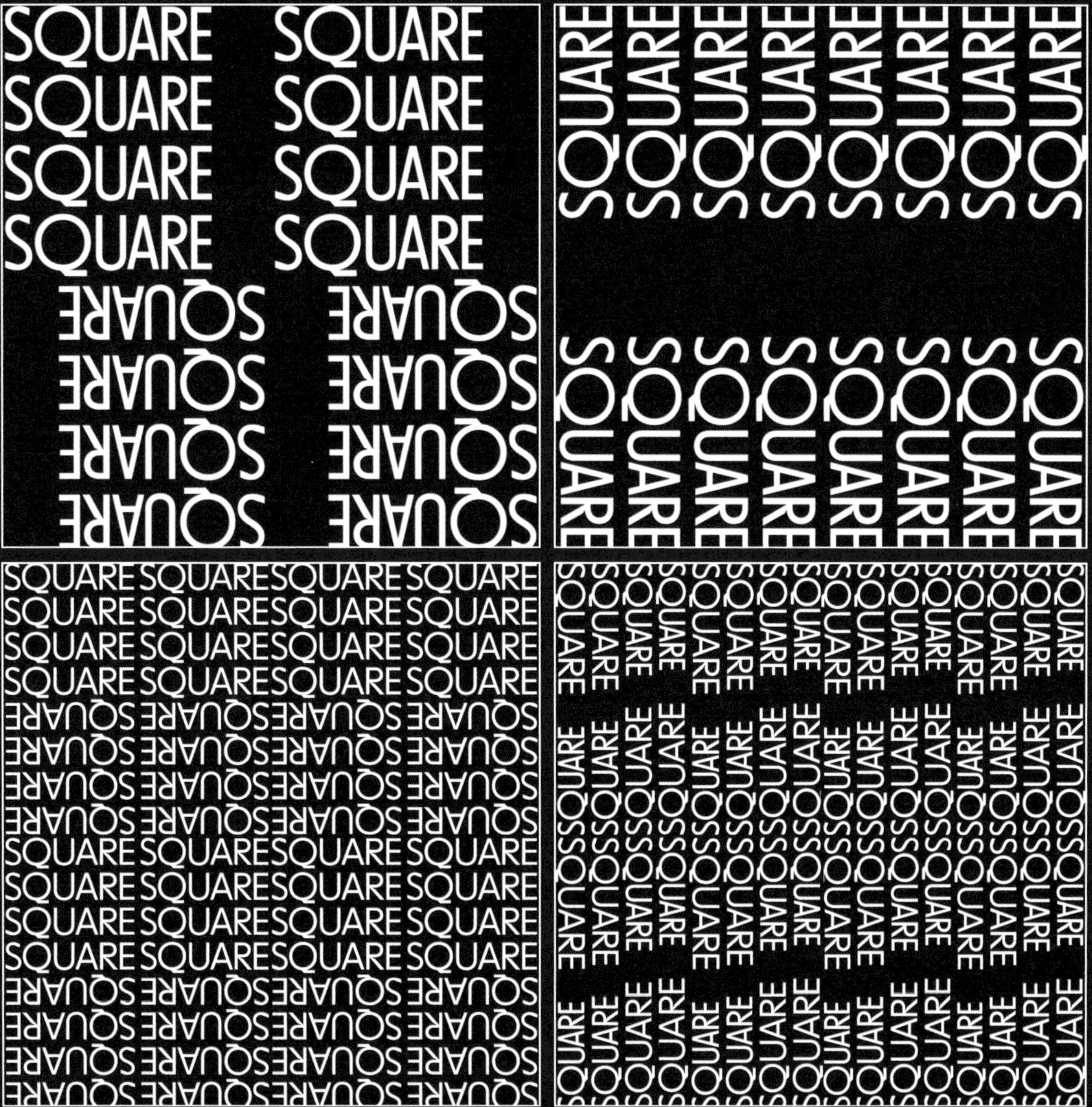

you use the walls as formats? Or not? What do you do? How do you make the text more interesting on the walls? You have new opportunities. There are new questions coming up, which I find fascinating from a research standpoint. Let's see where it goes.

3

ML: Is this what the augmented reality experiment "Bauhaus" was about?

MP: Yes, this is exactly what this was for. A practical, straightforward solution for exhibition typography. I think that of all the experiments we did, this might have been one of the most important ones. I could see an institution funding applications for that. It would actually save them money, and be more sustainable than printing vinyls over and over again.

Another application I see are exhibition spaces. You could literally just exhibit the work. The explanatory texts could be hidden in augmented reality. You could completely focus on the work and generate a design narrative. That could be an interesting investment for a museum.

ML: It is still special that DIA combines so many different skills. Do you think that your skillset will become the standard skillset of graphic design?

MP: I think it has to. Motion design is a very close discipline to graphic design and should be a part of the curriculum of any designer moving forward. It should not even be an elective subject for designers. It should be obligatory. As long as designers do not have at least a basic understanding of these relatively similar disciplines, then their output is going to stay the same. It is going to come from a traditional typographic understanding.

A lot of design firms produce very similar work. We have an internal joke where we switch the studios names and body of work. It just looks the same, even though it might be really great work. This is because students are not exposed to crafts other than their own in design schools.

If I could start a school, I would teach a wide range of disciplines. It is not about teaching them everything, but just enough to give you the ability to work with people who are better than you at those things. If you have no understanding about these things, it is difficult to collaborate with someone. You would give someone a logo and say, "animate that" without understanding that the concept of motion has ever been there to begin with. It will just look like it gets wiped on and off.

If a designer is not able to search for solutions outside of his core discipline, their solutions will always be typical. Anything can be a solution to a communication problem. For us, music can be a solution and visual effects can be a solution too. You are not able to think of these options if you have not exposed to these disciplines yourself. The most interesting work comes from the most unrelated connections. I do not understand how designers can reference other designers' work. There is so much other sh*t out there. You do not need to have a look at this other branding project. Do not do it. We do not do this in our office. We look at anything that is not in our core profession as inspiration. It makes things more interesting.

ML: I agree, but it is easier said than done. You need to be open for the new and the old, within and outside of your discipline. If it goes further than just changing your perspective and approach to the design problem, students can become overwhelmed by the challenges that come with coding or animation, apart from the other core skills a designer should have.

MP: Yes, it is a tricky thing. I went back to school to study frameworks with Zach (Lieberman). I cannot write frameworks at all. I knew I needed it because I cannot code in a creative sense, but the process of that work changed the game for me and how I operate existing software that I know. I understand now that I do not actually need to be able to code, but I need to be able to put my brain into their brain in that moment and then apply that thinking into what I do. This is different to "everyone needs to know everything". No! I think you need to know enough of what this specialist does, because it alters your approach. It also provides you with a lot of empathy for the specialist.

The fact that I went into the dark hole of learning type design gave me an incredible amount of respect for type designers. Selecting the right font could be the end goal. You do not need to mess with it because the type designer already had spend 8 years working on it. It is perfect. You do not have to be a master in everything, but you have to invest in the collaborative effort and the dialogue, then the outcome becomes much better.

It is tricky. You have to hand over trust, but you have to know what is for you and what is not. I know that coding is not for me. You need patience and I like to have immediate results. I like the idea that I can think like someone who codes and

3   Zach Lieberman (http://thesystemis.com) is
an artist, lecturer, researcher and developer.
He is the co-creator of openFrameworks, an
open source C++ toolkit for creative coding.

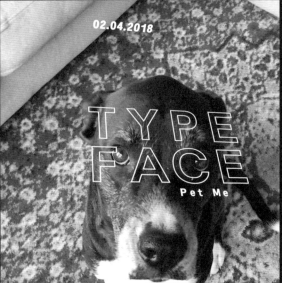

pilot some non-traditional solutions, but that is it. There is also something humbling in going into this painful situation, knowing that you will suck at this and that this is not for you, but I think that this is very important, because if you do not do this, you remain in this very controlled box of your limits. This is something I would totally recommend. Just give it a shot, even if you know that this is not for you. An inquisitive mentality is super important.

ML: Can you tell me a bit more about how trying to learn to code changed your mindset or how to approach or use your existing software?

MP: It was huge when I learned how generative systems behave. That was when I really learned how to connect the dots. I mean I always knew how similar music and design were, especially in animation. It is always rhythm and motion. When I saw that everything can be broken down to formulas, I thought, "oh sh*t!". Everything, I mean down to the animation behaviour, becomes trigonometry. Everything becomes developable in a way.

Once I started to think that this could be identity design, it was like, "holy sh*t!". It blew my mind. If you look at sheet music, it is just a looping system of coordinated elements. It really is just a formula. When you look into bio-mechanical structures and break them down, you have identifiers for everything. Every single thing that is here, that we see, gets kind of crazy and scientific, but it opens up the ball game. Someone's dance moves, if you simplify that into loopable behaviour, can become a visible identifier. So, that is a concept that could potentially be explored for a design piece. Everything is just a bunch of code. It really is just a formula. Then, it really reiterates a generative process. It is not about automating stuff. It is about getting rid of a lot of stuff that you would not want to do by hand and allow you to be more curatorial about the outcome. Let's try this at 10, or -10 and see what happens. Like a musician testing out. Tweaking the instrument. It was there, but I never really thought about it. An amplifier is nothing else than a bunch of code. Adobe Illustrator is really just the front end of code. It opened up a lot of windows for me.

On top of this, you can really stretch the limits of where your inspiration comes from. A running horse for example, the Eadweard Muybridge reference, becomes a very viable research interest for a designer now. The font as a variable, the sound as a variable, the motion as a variable, the colour as a variable, all the traditional design assets as variables – even behaviour could be the thing that locks it all down together or creates the visual form overall. A lot of our research revolves around this idea where behaviour can be the core concept for large corporate identity programmes. If you have an animation, all the printed deliverables are the last on the list. Take a millisecond of that animation and you have a poster. Done.

ML: Thanks so much, Mitch!
MP: Thank you!

Work
025

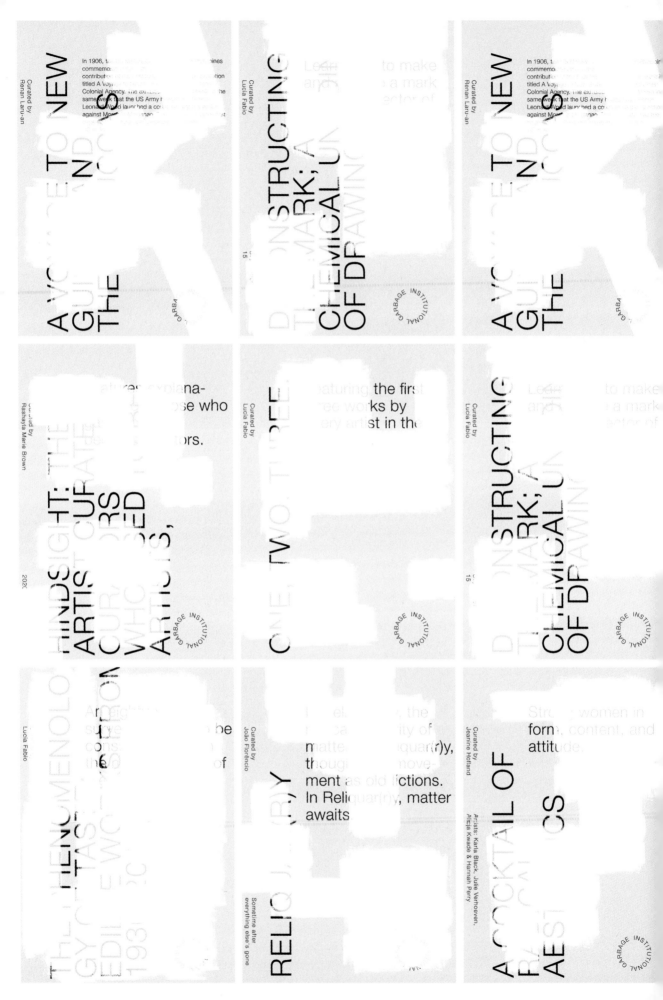

A VOYAGE TO NEW AND GUI The
Curated by Renan Laru-an

In 1906, ... combines commemo... contributo... tion titled A Voy... Colonial Agency. The ex... same week that the US Army ... Leonard Wood launched a co... against Mo... ...ao

DE/CONSTRUCTING THE MARK; A CHEMICAL UN OF DRAWING
Curated by Lucia Fabio
Lear and ... to make a mark ... actor of
15

GARBAGE INSTITUTIONAL

HINDSIGHT: THE ARTIST CURATE RS CUR ORS WHO SED ARTIS,
Curated by Rashayla Marie Brown
2020
...es explana- ...se who ...ors.

ONE, TWO, THREE.
Curated by Lucia Fabio
...aturing the first ...ee works by ...ery artist in the

THE PHENOMENOLO GY OF TAS EDI E WO ...RO 193
Lucia Fabio
A ...g ...sur... ...ons... ...he ...the ...of

RELIQ... (R)Y
Curated by João Florêncio
I ...el ... the ...ca... ity of matte... ...quar(r)y, thoug... ...nove ment as old ...ictions. In Reliquar(r)y, matter awaits
Sometime after everything else's gone

A COCKTAIL OF R AI AES CS
Curated by Jeanne Holland
Artists: Karla Black, Julie Verhoeven, Alicja Kwade & Hannah Perry
Stro... women in form, content, and attitude.

GARBAGE INSTITUTIONAL

Institutional Garbage
2017 — Poster
Client: The Green Lantern Press / Sector 2337
Typeface: Helvetica Neue
(Max Miedinger and Linotype Design Studio)
Design: Pouya Ahmadi

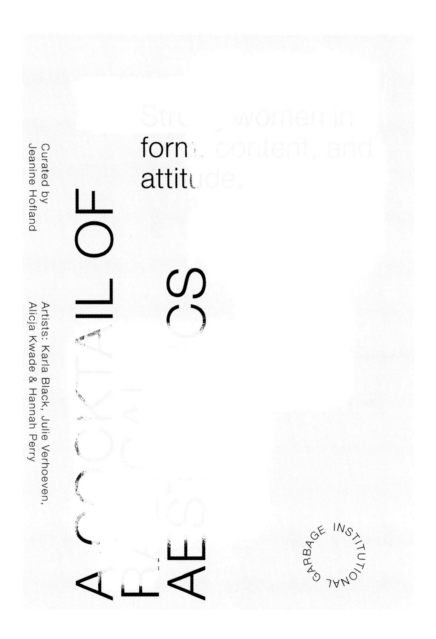

Institutional Garbage is an online exhibition that presents the administrative residue of imaginary public institutions produced by artists, writers, and curators. This residue that is not limited to contracts, includes email correspondences, documented unproductivity, syllabi, scanned objects, and obstacle courses. Collecting such fragments in one place, Institutional Garbage illustrates the backend activities of imaginary bureaucracies in an effort to trace the private lives of institutional endeavours. What comes to the fore is not a cohesive, singular agenda, but instead a cross-section of often misfired objects that, once assembled, try to tease out new strategies for community arts production, education, sustainability, and value assessment.

Retina N°03
Retina N°03
Retina N°03
Retina N°03
Retina N°03
Retina N°03
N°03
N°03
N°03
N°03
N°03

Roger Serret i Ricou
Christophe Synak
Guillermo Roca
Raphael López
Jose Porroche
Noé de López
Pau Sampera
Zgiim Elshani
Octave Abaji
Rose Guitian
Nepheli Nyx
Josh Payne
Diego Diez
Maria Nolla
Miguelito
Koln st.
Geray

Retina
Retina
Retina
Retina
Retina
Retina
Retina
Retina N°03
Retina –

Retina N°03

OT301
2nd Floor

European Videoart
Screenrecording
19 February
19:00 / 21:00
+ After Party

Cinema

2016
2016

Overtoom 301 - Amsterdam
European videoart & music
screen sessions.

Retina N°03

The Very Best of our Screens
The Very Best of our Screens
The Very Best of our Screens
The Very Best of our Screens
The Very Best of our Screens
The Very Best of our Screens
The Very Best of our Screens
The Very Best of our Screens
The Very Best of our Screens
The Very Best of our Screens
The Very Best of our Screens
The Very Best of our Screens
The Very Best of our Screens
The Very Best of our Screens
The Very Best of our Screens
The Very Best of our Screens
The Very Best of our Screens

European videoart & music
screen sessions. –

Retina N°03

The only video art !!!!!!!!!!!!!!!!!!!
screening night NOW !!!!!!!!!!!!!!
in Amsterdam - OT301 !!!!!!!!!!!!!!
!!
!!
!!
!!
!!
!!
!!
!!
!!
!!
!!
!!
!!

European videoart & music
screen sessions.

Retina
2016 — Campaign
Client: Geray Mena,
Olivia Lorraine, Koln Studio

Typeface:
Helvetica TI
(Max Miedinger, Adobe)
Design: Koln Studio

A platform for cultural promotion based on contemporary visual culture was born as a collective experimental exhibition by visual artist Geray Mena, cultural manager Olivia Lorraine, and Koln Studio. This project generated several events where different visual artists' creations were projected and curated, with each creation being an unpublished and unreleased piece exclusive to each event.

RETINA Nº04: Part of the 2016 Libros Mutantes Art Book Fair programme in Madrid, this event curated five-minute recordings of different artists' personal cell phones. RETINA Nº03: At OT301/ Overtoom 301/1054 HW in Amsterdam, several artists were invited to create an audiovisual piece featuring a 10-minute recording of their personal computer screens.

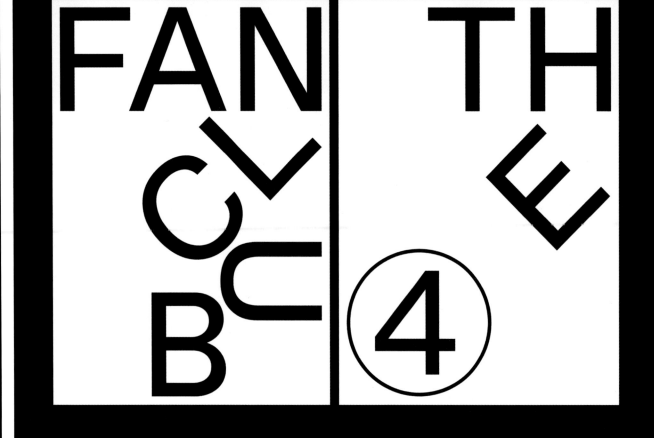
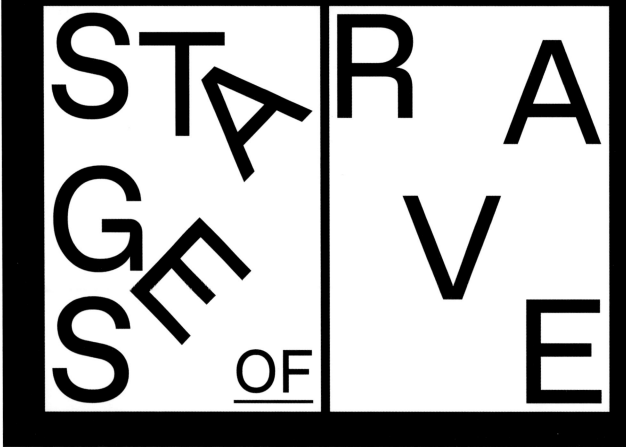

FanClub
2017 — Visual Identity

C l i e n t : F a n C l u b

Typeface: Favorit (Johannes Breyer and Fabian Harb, Dinamo)
Design: Ccccccitizon

Focusing on the scope of experiential innovation relat-
ing to the performance, transmission, and production
of music and neighbouring creative oulets, FanClub's
visual identity reflects adaptation through a polymer of
careful effortlessness and the consideration of context.

LE LE VE
LE LE VE
LE LE VE
LE LET'S RAVE
LET'S RAVE
LET'S RAVE
LET'S RAVE
FAN CLUB©

32.4042°S   152.2093°E

LE   VE
LE   VE
LE   VE
LE   VE
LE   VE
LE   VE
LE   VE
LE   VE
LE   VE 
FAN CLUB©

32.4042°S   152.2093°E

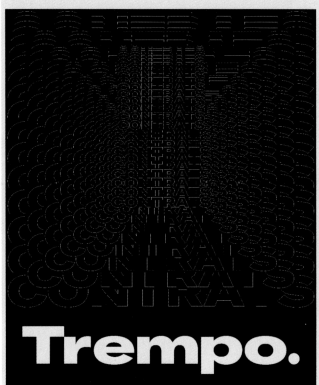

Trempo s2017
2017 — Visual Identity
Client: Trempolino
Typeface: GT America
(Noël Leu and Seb McLauchlan, Grilli Type)

Design: M   u   r   m   u   r   e

Trempo, a music campus and coaching platform in Nantes, selected Murmure to fully redesign its visual identity and entire communication media. For the first year of their collaboration, Murmure created a seasonal graphic universe built around a scalable typographic game based on keywords characterising Trempo's website activity and range of services.

Poster Collection
2018 — Posters
Typeface: Custom
Design: Fabian Fohrer

These posters are a small collection of re-interpreted store signs and commercial posters that were found in Providence, Rhode Island.

M2 Museologists

2018 — Visual Identity

Client: Valia Amoiridou
and George Adamidis

Typeface: sm Maxéville
(Mark Niemeijer), gfs Didot
(Greek Font Society, Google Fonts)
Design: Semiotik /
Dimitris Koliadimas

Contemporary museological reality is shaped by qualities associated with the tasks of studying, recording, highlighting, and documenting. As such, building a collection, conducting research, and conceptual museum planning are all expressions of a well-trained museologist's competence, and an opportunity to expand their skillset further. This brochure/ résumé embodies all these qualities and skills as manifested in the careers and cultural experiences of museologist-curators and long-term collaborators, George Adamidis and Valia Amoiridou. The design was "curated" to reflect their body of work and maximise visual impact, even though it was produced on a very minimal printing budget.

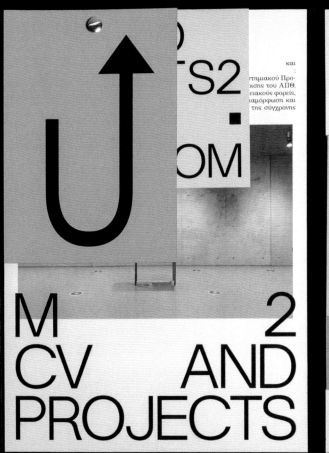

B BBB
Â TTT
  TTT

A
R D

www ● batard ◯ be
www ● beursschouwburg ◯ be
facebook.com/batardfestival

BÂTARD
BÂTARD

Opening up   a larger space
(which is uncertain in its nature
&   direction)

www   ●   batard   ◯   be

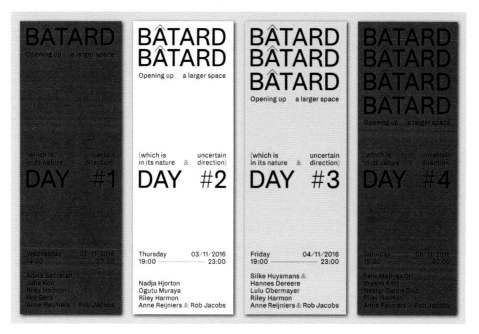

Bâtard 2016
2016 — Visual Identity
Client: Bâtard Festival (Brussels)
Typeface: Dia (Florian Schick and Lauri Toikka, Schick Toikka)

Design:

Ines Cox, Ward Heirwegh

Ines Cox and Ward Heirwegh created this visual identity for the 2016 Bâtard Festival in Brussels. The subtitle of this specific edition, "opening up a larger space (which is uncertain in its nature & direction)", generated a form of dynamic visual play, where various zones within the different communication materials could shift and transform constantly.

Sprengel Museum Hannover
Dezember 2017

Sprengel Museum Hannover
April 2018

Sprengel Museum Hannover
Maerz 2018

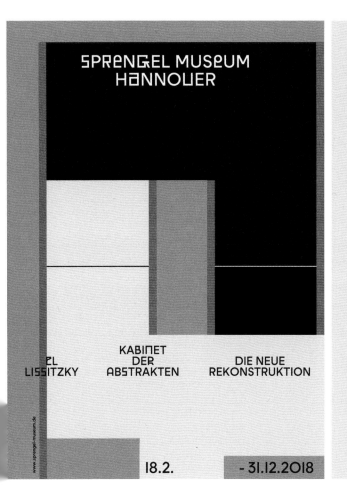
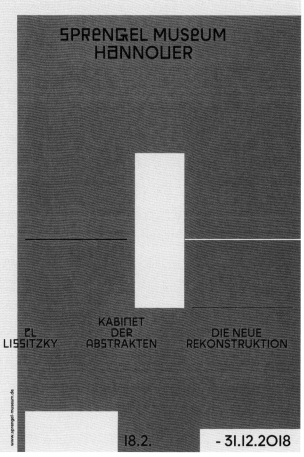

Sprengel Museum Hannover
2017 — Visual Identity
Client: Sprengel Museum Hannover
Typeface: Kurt (David Turner)

Design:

Bureau

Bordeaux

+

David

Turner

In 2017, Bureau Bordeaux were tasked to create a new visual identity for Sprengel Museum Hannover, a famous museum of modern arts that opened in 1979. Its building complex had expanded multiple times over the years to make way for a constantly growing collection. To reflect this, the studio worked with David Turner to create an evolving Lego-like typeface that referenced the Architype Schwitters font.

HERZOG & DE MEURON OCT 8 6PM

SPRING LECTURE 2014

IIT ARCHITECTURE CHICAGO S. R. CROWN HALL

ALL LECTURES ARE BOTH FREE AND PUBLIC. MORE INFO AT: ARCH.IIT.EDU

IIT College of Architecture

EDWARD UHLIR NOV 19 6PM

SPRING LECTURE 2014

IIT ARCHITECTURE CHICAGO S. R. CROWN HALL

PRINCIPAL, RAFAEL VINOLY ARCHITECTS

DESIGNING THE TALLEST RESIDENTAL BUILDING IN THE WESTERN HEMISPHERE: 432 PARK AVENUE

ALL LECTURES ARE BOTH FREE AND PUBLIC. MORE INFO AT: ARCH.IIT.EDU

STAN ALLEN FEB 12 6PM

IIT ARCHITECTURE CHICAGO S. R. CROWN HALL

PRINCIPAL SAAYSTAN ALLEN ARCHITECT NEW YORK

DESIGNING THE SMALLEST OFFICE BUILDING IN THE EAST: 234 WOOD STREET

SPRING LECTURES 2014

ALL LECTURES ARE BOTH FREE AND PUBLIC. MORE INFO AT ARCH.IIT.EDU

PIER PAOLO TAM— BURELLI

CLOUD TALKS 2014

MON, NOV 10 1:30 PM

PROJECT OF A HISTORICAL ARCHITECTURE

IIT ARCHITECTURE CHICAGO S. R. CROWN HALL LOWER CORE

Pier Paolo Tamburelli (Tortona, 1978) studied at the University of Genoa and at the Berlage Institute Rotterdam. In 2004 he founded the architecture office baukuh, together with Paolo Carpi, Silvia Lupi, Vittorio Pizzigoni, Giacomo Summa, and Andrea Zanderigo. Tamburelli took part in the exhibition "Monditalia (2008) and collaborated with baukuh at San PADAR la PAR la PAR. He has lectured at a number of schools and cultural institutions, including the Architectural Association, Cornell University, EPFL, Lausanne, FAU São Paulo, FFAR Stockholm, Hochgeturet Buchhandlung Zürich, IIT Chicago, IUAV Venice, Kunsthal Rotterdam, MAXXI Rome, RWTH Aachen, Tongji University Shanghai and the USI Mendrisio.

ARCH.IIT.EDU   IIT College of Architecture

EDUARD FUEHR

CLOUD TALKS 2014

WED, NOV 12 2:00 PM

BERLIN WALL CONSTRUCTION AND COGNITION 1952-2014

IIT ARCHITECTURE CHICAGO S. R. CROWN HALL LOWER CORE

Eduard Führ has been teaching and researching as a Professor of Theory of Architecture and Architectural History at various Universities, such as the Hochschule für Bremenen Cottbus, Hochschule Stuttgart, Brandenburgische Technische Universität Cottbus and the University of Minho Olonen.

Parallel to academia, Professor Führ also works as a consultant for construction and planning projects. In 1996, he founded Cloud-Cuckoo-Land, the bi-lingual online magazine published essence of Theory of Architecture in English, Russian and German. Professor Führ's body of research.

ARCH.IIT.EDU

LOUIS VUITTON SPARK AWARD

CLOUD EVENT 2015

MON, APR 5 6:30 PM

LOUIS VUITTON AND THE CITY OF CHICAGOOF CULTURAL

IIT ARCHITECTURE CHICAGO S. R. CROWN HALL LOWER CORE

The Louis Vuitton Spark Award, sponsored by Louis Vuitton and the City of Chicago's Department of Cultural Affairs and Special Events, honors an outstanding student from the College of Architecture's undergraduate and graduate Cloud-Studio program reflecting the College's focus on the City of Chicago and Bettered Metropolis." The recipient of the second year Vuitton SPARK Award will travel to Paris to meet with the Louis Vuitton architecture department responsible for the designs of Louis Vuitton boutiques around the world. The winning project will also be featured in an installation in the Louis Vuitton store on Michigan Avenue in Chicago later this summer.

ARCH.IIT.EDU   IIT College of Architecture

IIT ARCHITECTURE CHICAGO BIENNIAL PROGRAMS

CHICAGO

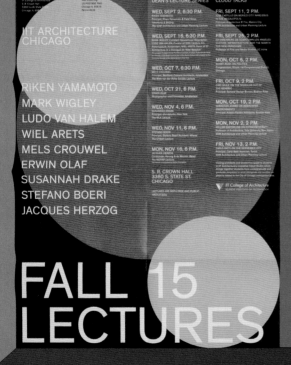

IIT ARCHITECTURE CHICAGO

RIKEN YAMAMOTO
MARK WIGLEY
LUDO VAN HALEM
WIEL ARETS
MELS CROUWEL
ERWIN OLAF
SUSANNAH DRAKE
STEFANO BOERI
JACQUES HERZOG

FALL LECTURES 15

CHICAGO ARCHI-TECTURE BIENNIAL

JACQUES HERZOG
THE MCHAP LECTURE
MON, NOV 16, 6 P.M.
S. R. CROWN HALL

Top poster (left)

OPEN
HOUSE

ANNUAL
STUDENT
EXHIBIT

FRI, MAY 8, 2015

5 P.M.
AWARD PRESENTATION

5:30—8 P.M.
OPEN HOUSE

Top poster (right)

IIT ARCHITECTURE
CHICAGO

WINY MAAS

JORGE FRANCISCO
LIERNUR

ADRIAAN GEUZE

MARCELO FERRAZ

WIEL ARETS

JOSHUA
PRINCE-RAMUS

BERNARD KHOURY

IWAN BAAN

SPRING 15
LECTURES

DEAN'S LECTURE SERIES

WED, FEB 4, 6 P.M.
MON, MAR 23, 6:30 P.M.
FRI, FEB 27, 6:30 P.M.
WED, APR 1, 6:30 P.M.
WED, APR 22, 6:30 P.M.
THU, APR 23, 6:30 P.M.
FRI, MAY 8, 5 P.M.

S. R. CROWN HALL
3360 SOUTH STATE ST.
CHICAGO, IL 60616

LECTURES ARE BOTH
FREE AND PUBLIC
INFO: ARCH.IIT.EDU

CLOUD TALKS

MON, JAN 26, 2 P.M.
FRI, JAN 30, 2 P.M.
FRI, FEB 20, 2 P.M.
FRI, FEB 27, 2 P.M.
WED, MAR 4, 2 P.M.
FRI, MAR 6, 2 P.M.
MON, MAR 30, 2 P.M.
MON, APR 13, 2 P.M.
WED, APR 15, 2 P.M.
THU, APR 16, 2 P.M.
FRI, APR 17, 2 P.M.

Bottom poster (left)

IIT ARCHITECTURE
CHICAGO

WILLIAM BAKER
DAVID ADJAYE
ARMAND MEVIS
LINDA VAN DEURSEN
CRAIG DYKERS
JEAN PIERRE CROUSSE
FLORENCIA RODRIGUEZ
JACQUES HERZOG
VITTORIO LAMPUGNANI

SPRING 16
LECTURES
& EVENTS

DEAN'S LECTURE SERIES

FRI, JAN 15, 6 P.M.
MON, FEB 15, 6 P.M.
WED, FEB 17, 6 P.M.
FRI, FEB 19, 6 P.M.
WED, MAR 2, 6 P.M.
MON, MAR 7, 6:30 P.M.
WED, MAR 30, 6:90 P.M.

S. R. CROWN HALL
3360 S. STATE ST.
CHICAGO

CLOUD TALKS

FRI, JAN 29, 2 P.M.
FRI, FEB 22, 6:30 P.M.
FRI, FEB 26, 2 P.M.
MON, MAR 21, 2 P.M.
FRI, APR 22, 2 P.M.

EVENTS

FRI, MAR 4–SAT, MAR 5
THU, MAR 31, 6 P.M.
FRI, APR 1
FRI, MAY 13, 5 P.M.

Bottom poster (right)

THE
AMERICAS
PRIZE
2014/15

MIES CROWN HALL
AMERICAS PRIZE
MCHAP.ORG

MCHAP.EMERGE
SYMPOSIUM
FRI, APR 1

MCHAP EXHIBITION
FRI, MAR 4–
SAT, MAR 5

S. R. CROWN HALL
3360 S. STATE ST.
CHICAGO, IL 60616

IIT
Architecture Chicago

2014 – 2017
Visual Identity

Client:
IIT Architecture Chicago

Typeface:
Theinhardt (Francois Rappo, Optimo)

Design:
Mainstudio / Edwin Van Gelder

Mainstudio's graphic poster system for IIT Architecture Chicago's lecture posters features four varying "information zones" alongside contrasting colours and dots as the basic organisational components. The dots are patterned to create forms in varying colours and sizes, while the typeface used reflects the rigid grid system favoured by the school's founder, Mies van der Rohe. As such, bigger lecture posters could be further deconstructed into smaller ones seamlessly.

RÉALISATION DE SCÈNES
VENTE: ÉCLAIRAGE / SONORISATION / TECHNIQUES
DE SCÈNE / VIDÉO / PODIUM
LOCATION DE MATÉRIEL
ÉTUDES DE FAISABILITÉ DE PROJETS

SA

T

É

ÉCLAIRAGE THÉÂTRE SA
AVENUE DES BAUMETTES 15 — 1020 RENENS VD

SAMEDI
30 JUILLET
14 — 16H

SA

T

É

ÉCLAIRAGE THÉÂTRE
S'AGRANDIT À
NOUVEAU CET ÉTÉ

APÉRITIF 30 JUILLET
15H30 — 20H

VOUS ÊTES INVITÉ
À NOS JOURNÉES
PORTES OUVERTES
QUI SE TIENDRONT
À NOS BUREAUX
DE RENENS

ÉCLAIRAGE THÉÂTRE SA
AV. DES BAUMETTES 15 — 1020 RENENS VD
TEL. 021'637'72'25
WWW.ECLAIRAGE-THEATRE.CH

NOUVEAUTÉ
DIGITAL
SIGNAGE

SA

T

É

INFORMEZ EN
TEMPS RÉEL TOUS
VOS VISITEURS
DES NOUVEAUTÉS,
HORAIRES ET
PROCHAINES
REPRÉSENTATIONS

NOUS SOMMES LA
PREMIÈRE ENTRE-
PRISE DU MARCHÉ
À VOUS OFFRIR
LE SERVICE «DIGITAL
SIGNAGE»

ÉCLAIRAGE THÉÂTRE SA
AV. DES BAUMETTES 15 — 1020 RENENS VD
TEL. 021'637'72'25
PLUS D'INFOS: ECLAIRAGE-THEATRE.CH

RÉALISATION DE SCÈNES
VENTE: ÉCLAIRAGE / SONORISATION / TECHNIQUES
DE SCÈNE / VIDÉO / PODIUM
LOCATION DE MATÉRIEL
ÉTUDES DE FAISABILITÉ DE PROJETS

SA

T

É

ÉCLAIRAGE THÉÂTRE SA
AVENUE DES BAUMETTES 15 — 1020 RENENS VD

Éclairage Théâtre
2016 — Visual Identity
Client: Éclairage Théâtre sa
Typeface: Akzidenz Grotesk (Günter Gerhard Lange)

Design:

Bilal

Sebei

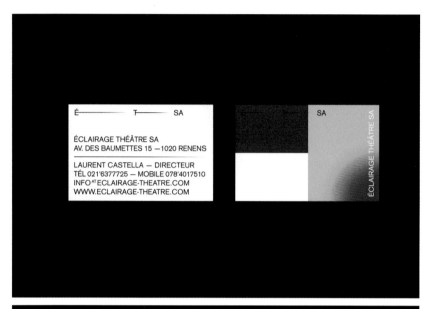

Éclairage Théâtre sa is a company specialising in lighting for scenography, theatres, television, discotheques, and concert halls. The goal of this proposal by Bilal Sebei was to totally rebrand its visual identity, with a design concept that revolved around representing light diffusion through space. Through the thoughtful use of three-dimensional spaces and colour, the designer sought to symbolise the essence of the company's work, which is to become invisible to the public eye and put the show at the forefront. By revealing what is usually not shown on stage, such as structures and sources of light, he hoped to deconstruct the too-technical image typically attributed to the company and evoke emotions in an abstract manner, leaving more room for imagination.

L'Arte

Artigiani: storie e
percorsi di qualità e
di eccellenza.

ARTE L'ARTE L'ARTE L'ARTE

dell'

Artigianato

Design: Brando Corradini

This project was not only inspired by craft, but also the art of making craft in itself. Brando Corradini's homeland, Italy, is among the few industrialised countries that continue to celebrate artisan workshops and traditions today, where their excellence in manual production is recognised worldwide.

52

Rundgang HGB 2016
2016 — Poster (DIN A0, DIN A1)
Client: Hochschule für Grafik und Buchkunst
Typeface: Aktuell,

A   k   z   i   d   e   n   z   Grotesk
(Günter Gerhard Lange)
Design: Lamm & Kirch

These posters were designed for the Annual Exhibition of the Hochschule für
Grafik und Buchkunst Academy of Fine Arts Leipzig.

Migrant Journal
2016 to present — Publication
Client: Migrant Journal Press
Typeface: Migrant Grotesk (Offshore Studio),
Akzidenz Grotesk (Günter Gerhard Lange)

Design:
O
f
f
s
h
o
r
e
Studio

MIGRANT JOURNAL explores the circulation of people, goods, information, as well as flora and fauna around the world; and the transformative impact it has on space. While migration is part of humanity's genesis, it seems as though the phenomenon has become ubiquitous and is happening faster than ever, with complex ramifications.

Yves Bachmann
2015 — Visual Identity
Client: Yves Bachmann
Typeface: FF Bau
(Christian Schwartz, FontFont)

Design:

Kevin

Hoegger

Kevin Hoegger designed this visual identity for Swiss photographer Yves Bachmann in 2015. The idea was to only use colour and type as key visual elements to communicate information and let the photographs speak for themselves. Together, they created two different book series: Diary and Images. Diary consisted of the photographer's daily photo album, whereas Images formed his commercial portfolio. While the books shared the same cover page layout, they sported different colour combinations and different contents.

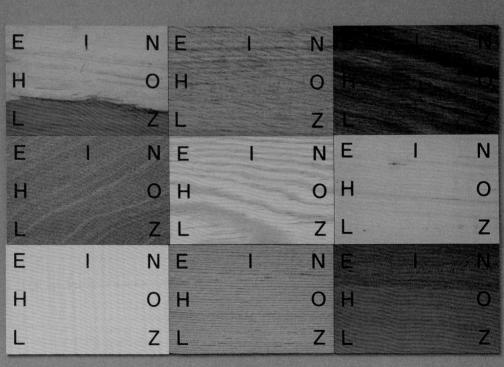

Einholz
2014 — Visual Identity
Client: Einholz

Typeface: Favorit   (Johannes   Breyer   and   Fabian   Harb,   Dinamo)

Design: Bureau Collective

Ueli Reusser specialises in woodwork and founded his own one-man join-
ery in 2014. The name "Einholz" was derived from "Einhorn" ("unicorn"
in English) and underlines his specialisation as an independent carpenter.
The flexible design grid in his visual identity stands for his wide range of
tasks, and can be applied to any rectangular shape. His business cards are
made from real wood out of his archive, making each one truly unique.

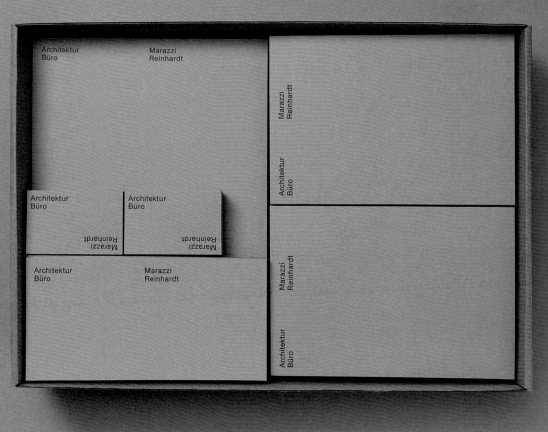

2012 — Visual Identity
Client: Marazzi Reinhardt
Typeface: Union (Radim Peško)
Design: Bureau Collective

Sergio Marazzi and Andreas Reinhardt are two talented architects based in Winterthur, who founded their own studio, Brand 3, in 2002. For its 10th anniversary, they sought to develop a new, grown-up visual identity and decided to rename it to Marazzi Reinhardt after a period of intense evaluation and analysis.

    Sergio and Andreas' work is characterised by the use of raw materials throughout their projects, where they stage and transform every object under an urban light by seamlessly integrating the environment and understanding how to combine existing elements with the new. Due to this meaningful approach, Bureau Collective's design concept for the visual identity was based on a very simple, clear, and flexible grid. Doing without a logo for a sense of authenticity, each branded collateral was divided down the middle to define the position of the text or respective title in a consistent manner. Besides a timeless font in only two sizes, a warm grey tone was also applied throughout the concept, including the studio space, for cohesion. Material-wise, a customised corporate paper made in collaboration with Gmund Paper was used for printed matter, including envelopes, to ensure co-ordination between all the stationery.

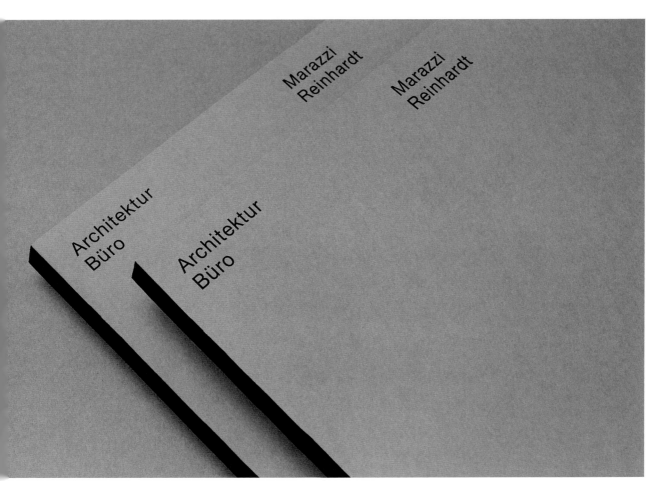

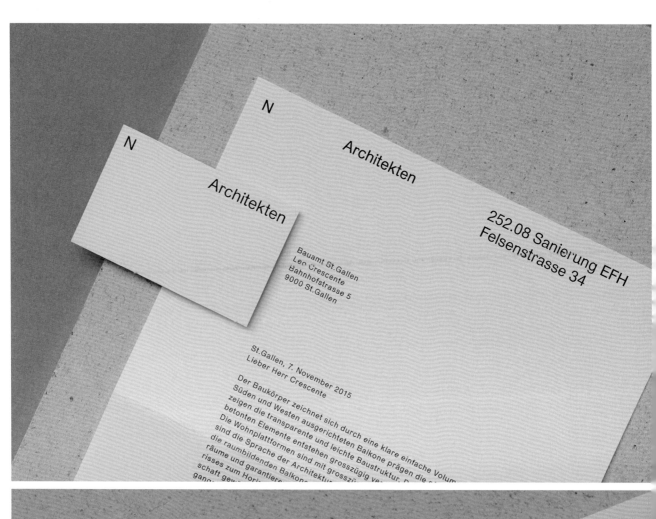

N

Architekten

N

Architekten

252.08 Sanierung EFH
Felsenstrasse 34

Bauamt St. Gallen
Leo Crescente
Bahnhofstrasse 5
9000 St. Gallen

St. Gallen, 7. November 2015
Lieber Herr Crescente

Der Baukörper zeichnet sich durch eine klare einfache Volum
Süden und Westen ausgerichteten Balkone prägen die
zeigen die transparente und leichte Baustruktur. D
betonten Elemente entstehen grosszügig ve
Die Wohnplattformen sind mit grosszügig
sind die Sprache der Architektu
die raumbildenden Balkone
räume und garantiere
risses zum Hori
schaft gew
gang

Architekten

N

2015 — Visual Identity
Client: Niedermann Architekten
Typeface: Hansruedi (Samuel Bänziger)
Design: Bureau Collective

In collaboration with Niedermann Architekten, an architecture studio based in St. Gallen, Bureau Studio developed an identity system that could easily be handled and maintained by the client independently. To reflect the succession of duties from the previous managing director (Urs Niedermann) to the new one, the design continued to feature the studio name as a fundamental element, but with a slight tweak – the reduction of the word "Niedermann" to simply "N". The white space in between the "N" and "Architekten" is defined by the exact width of letters missing from the original word.

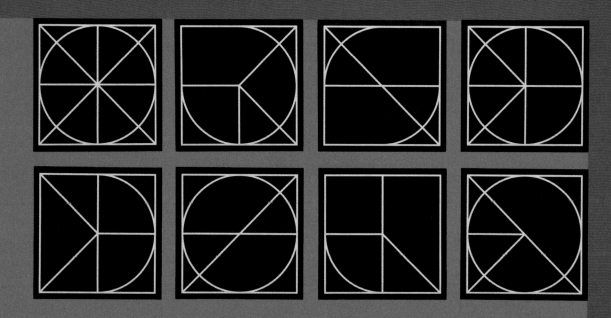

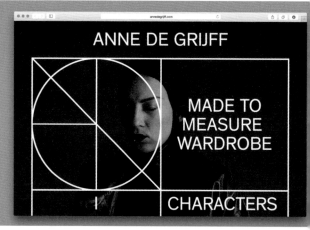

ANNE DE GRIJFF

MADE TO
MEASURE
WARDROBE

I   CHARACTERS

Christine
Vroom
Aynouk Tan
Tonny Jansen
Annelies v
Eenennaam
Mo Veld
→   Amie Dicke
Liesbeth List

II   WARDROBE

Anne de Grijff

2015 — Visual Identity

Client: Anne de Grijff

Typeface: Theinhardt

(Francois Rappo, Optimo)

Design: Mainstudio / Edwin Van Gelder

Anne de Grijff is a Dutch fashion designer. For her 2015 collection, where she created capsules for each of her "characters", her brand's visual identity system was centered upon the concept of made-to-measure, using "leather and jerseys, pure wool, luxurious synthetics, and fine silks". Reflecting that material palette was a flexible grid incorporating a square, circle, cross, and plus sign, and the framing bold lines of the identity's graphics could be deconstructed and reconfigured into countless compositions to create an infinite number of those shapes. This framework was also used as a template for the brand's other designed items, such as hang tags, bags, and stationery.

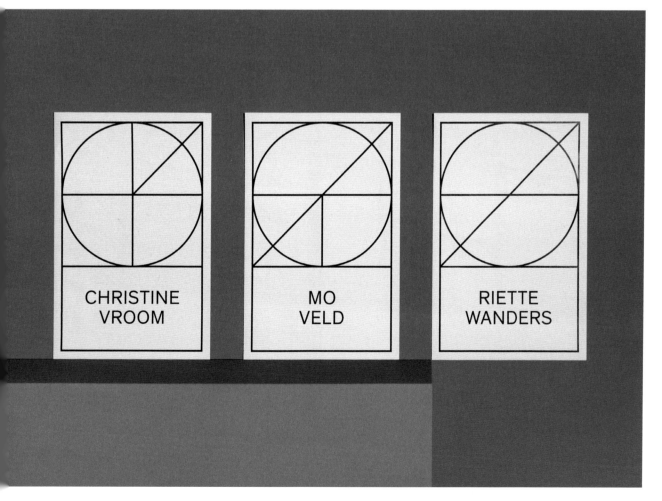

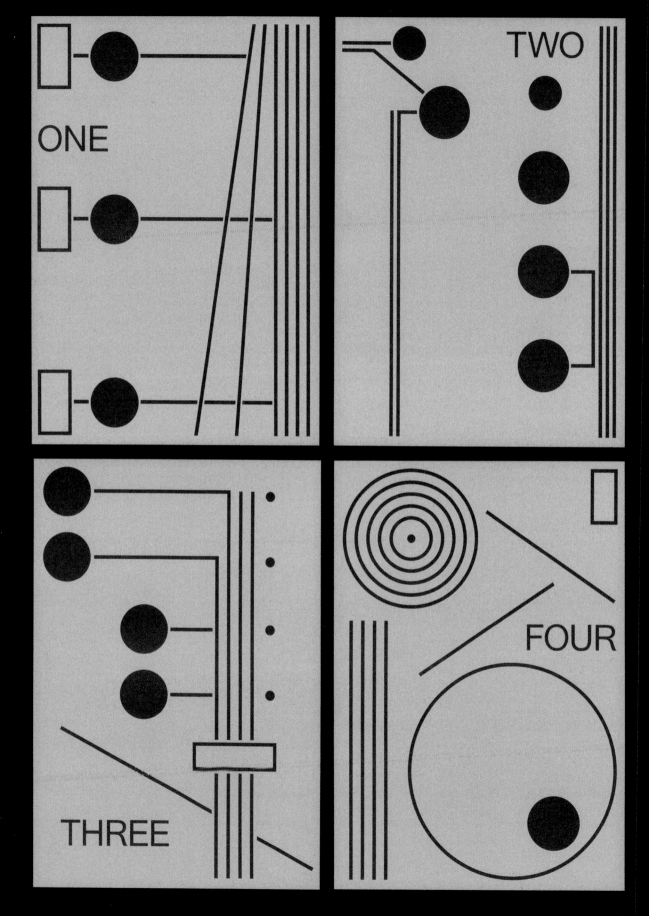

Client: District Five

Typeface: Union (Radim Peško)   Design: Offshore Studio

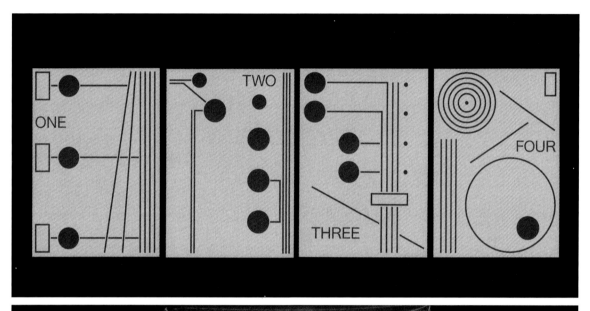

For Zurich-based jazz band District Five Quartet's identity system, the visual language for the website, flyers, and programmes makes use of the visual codes and symbols found in music, as well as the four instruments used by the band.

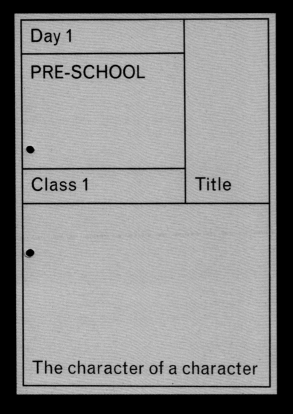

Day 1

PRE-SCHOOL

●

| Class 1 | Title |

●

The character of a character

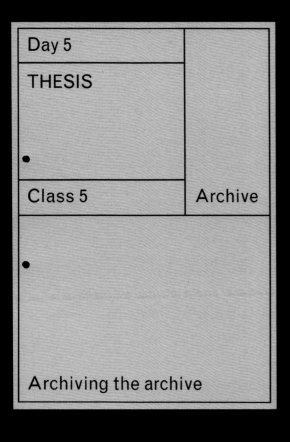

Day 5

THESIS

●

| Class 5 | Archive |

●

Archiving the archive

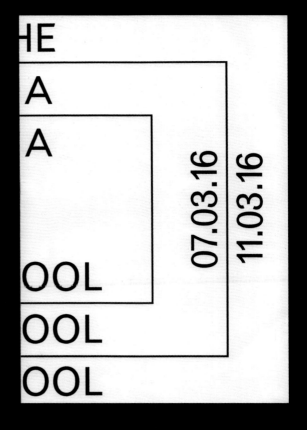

HE

A

A

07.03.16

11.03.16

OOL

OOL

OOL

in a SCHOOL   in a SCHOOL

2016 — Workshop
Client: ISBA (Besançon)
Typeface: Grotesque MT (Frank Hinman)
Design: Ines Cox

Day 3	
MIDDLE SCHOOL	
●	
Class 3	Page
●	
The story in a story	

This is the documentation that resulted from a four-day workshop guided by Ines Cox at ISBA Besançon in 2016, where the
students worked on various typographic interpretations of
Raymond Queneau's Exercises in Style.

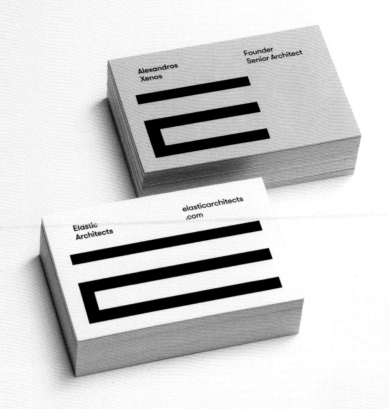

2018 — Visual Identity
Client: Elastic Architects
Typeface: GT Haptik
(Reto Moser and Tobias Rechsteiner, Grilli Type)
Design: Semiotik / Dimitris Koliadimas

**elastic
architects
.com**

ELASTIC

Semiotik were commissioned to create a brand new identity for
Elastic Architects, a group of architects and international partners
who experiment with boundaries and believe in the flexibility
of manufacturing innovation. Working on the notion of the word
"elastic" and starting with the form of the letter "E", they created
a dynamic identity system that served the primary design objectives of clarity, functionality, and flexibility.

BIT R0T

Published on the occasion of the exhibition *Bit Rot* at
Witte de With Center for Contemporary Art, Rotterdam, 2015

Short Stories and Essays
Douglas Coupland

Douglas Coupland
Bit Rot
11 September 2015 – 3 January 2016

Opening:
Thursday 10 September 2015, 5pm

With *Bit Rot*, artist and novelist Douglas Coupland shares his
thoughts on globalization, terror, the Internet, pop-culture, social
media and the resulting accelerated image economy. Taking its title
from the phenomenon in which digital data spontaneously and
quickly decomposes, Bit Rot creates an associative and visually
playful constellation in which memory, loss, fame, destruction,
and creation are subjects for contemplation.

The exhibition presents Coupland's 'mindscape', combining
his own work with loans from his personal collection, as well
as new work stemming from his recent residency at the Google
Cultural Institute. An eponymous paperback collection of
new and existing short stories and essays written and compiled
by the artist will accompany the exhibition.

Curators: Defne Ayas, Samuel Saelemakers

The exhibition marks the start of Futurosity, which is part of Rotterdam viert de stad!
and is kindly supported by the city of Rotterdam and The Art of Impact.

Exhibition supported by

INTRACORP   A O D O M

Witte de With   T +31 (0)10 4110144
Center for Contemporary Art   F +31 (0)10 4117924
Witte de Withstraat 50
3012 BR Rotterdam   info@wdw.nl
The Netherlands   www.wdw.nl

Witte de With
Contemporary Art

Douglas Coupland: Bit Rot
2015 — Publication
Client: Witte de With Center for Contemporary Art

Typeface:
Custom GT Cinetype (Mauro Paolozzi and Rafael Koch Grilli Type),
Regular (Henrik Kubel, A2-Type), Catull (Gustav Jaeger),
Helvetica Neue (Max Miedinger and Linotype Design Studio),
Times New Roman (Stanley Morison)
Design: A Practice for Everyday Life

Douglas Coupland's first major solo exhibition in Europe was held at Witte de With Center for Contemporary Art in Rotterdam in the autumn of 2015. The show combined Coupland's own work with loans from his personal collection, creating a rich tapestry of associations and stories that collectively addressed themes such as globalisation, terror, pop culture, the internet, and social media. This publication was designed to accompany the exhibition—containing a collection of Coupland's stories and essays. The typographic cover design made reference to the book's title, Bit Rot, which is a term used to describe the degeneration of digital software over time. The typography and layouts were evocative of early computer bit fonts and displays, with the texts presented in a continuous stream, only interrupted by seemingly random changes in typefaces, paper stock, and typographic glitches.

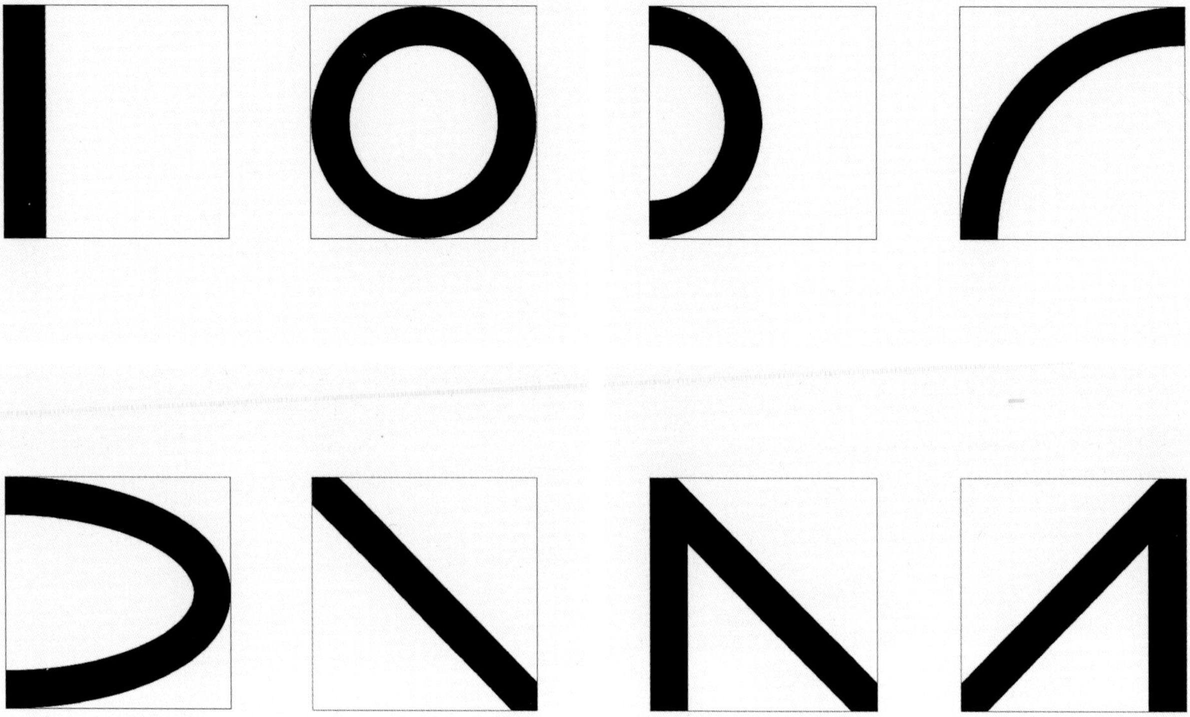

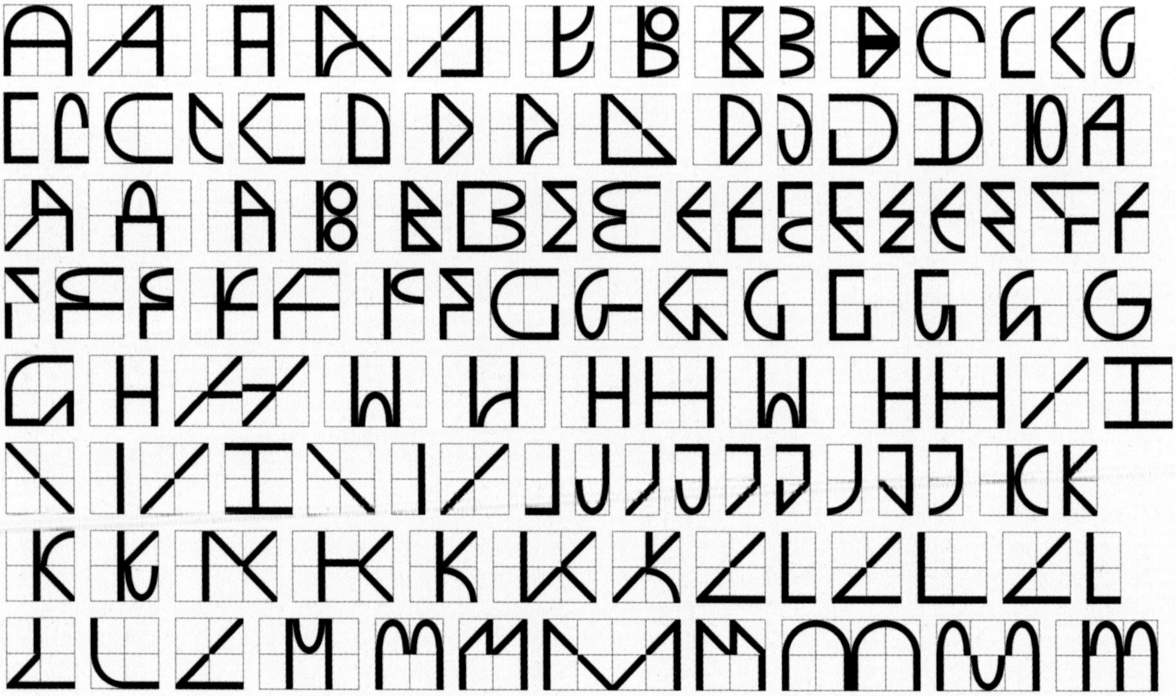

2016 — Typeface
Typeface: Galapagos (Felix Salut, Dinamo)
Design: Felix Salut and Dinamo

The Galapagos Typeface is based on the Galapagos Game invented by Felix Salut, which was used as a prop for his 2014 short film, Shut Up I'm Counting. The script-turned-book, published by Spector Books, was awarded the Walter Tiemann Prize in the same year.

For the typeface, Felix Salut and Dinamo composed the same nine modules into seven alphabets of different styles: Rounded, Straight, Angular, Rounded-Straight, Straight-Angular, Rounded Angular, and Rounded-Straight-Angular. The result is a total of 70 typefaces, where each style comes in five weights, with Grid and No-Grid versions. Using Stylistic Sets, all characters can be moved up and down along the vertical grid.

Just as the Galapagos Islands are home to a vast number of unique species, the Galapagos Typeface encompasses a range of characters whose forms evolve from one another.

Katharina
Gaenssler

Bauhaus
Staircase—

Dessau,
New York,
Tel Aviv.

2015/16.

VISUAL MUSIC AND MUSIC VIDEO SCREENING

GENERAL PUBLIC

BERLIN 20.10.1

This event is presented to you by KONOMONO www.monomono.ch

Date: Wednesday, October 20, 2012
Time: 23:00 PM - 4:00 AM
Location: Schönhauser Allee 167c
Berlin, U2 Senefelder Platz

Mono Mono
2016 — Poster

Typeface: Mono Mono
(Custom)

Design: Simon Mager

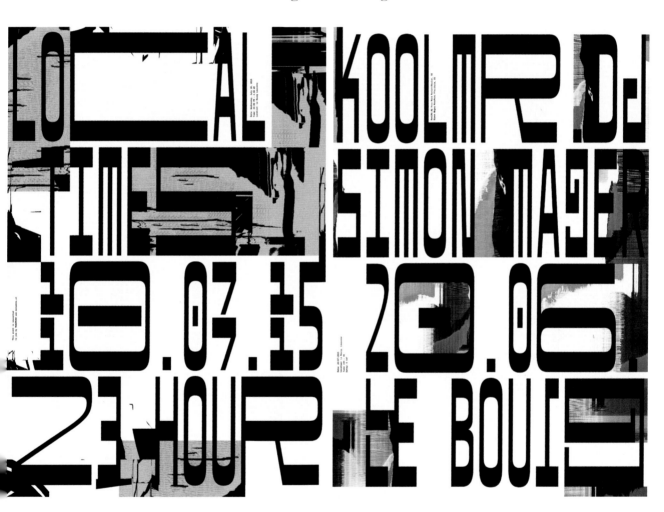

Mono Mono was a viral series of events that revolved around
the topic of music and visual culture. Its visual identity was
based on an expansive monospaced typeface drawn for the
series, paired with visuals created using a modified scanner.

Design: Simon Mager

This poster is a visual response to a photograph by Albert Elm, a Copenhagen-based photographer, featuring a tree mingling with a wall with its branches reaching through a purpose-built fence. A custom typeface was created to make up the rich visual details through morphing shapes.

Design: Fabian Fohrer

Exposit is a typeface that reinterprets Joseph A. David's Plaque Découpée Universelle, a stencil originally designed in 1876 to draw all letters, numbers, symbols and punctuations on the basis of its grid. Developed on a likewise grid system, Exposit's characters transmit a grid-based, constructed aesthetic. The display typeface is enhanced through the expression of its letterforms, which can be uniform and calm, but also irregular and turbulent. Similarly, the interplay of vertical stroke lengths, condensed and extended letters, as well as expansions of rounded shapes define Exposit's dynamic and changing characteristics.

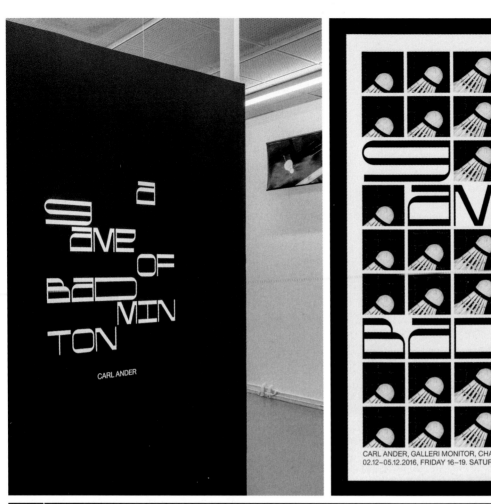

CARL ANDER

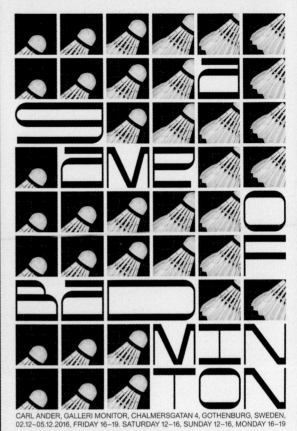

CARL ANDER, GALLERI MONITOR, CHALMERSGATAN 4, GOTHENBURG, SWEDEN, 02.12–05.12.2016, FRIDAY 16–19. SATURDAY 12–16, SUNDAY 12–16, MONDAY 16–19

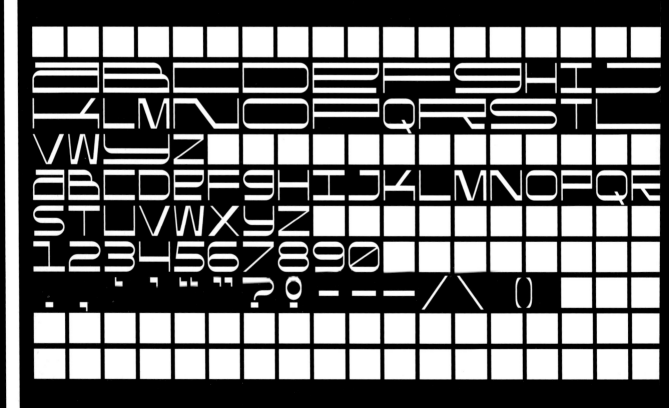

A   Game   of   Badminton

2016 — Visual Identity

Client: Monitor   Art   Gallery

Typeface: Bad Mono (Custom)

Design: Tor   Weibull

Photographer Carl Ander's A Game of Badminton exhibition at the Monitor Art Gallery featured photography from a particular badminton match. Referencing this, Tor Weibull created a unique visual identity that worked around a clear grid reminiscent of the square-patterned net used in the game, while the high and low movements often made by players also became a big part of the inspiration in developing and drawing the custom typeface, Bad Mono, that was used throughout the exhibition collateral.
Photography: © Carl Ander

RENé
COU
LON

N°1

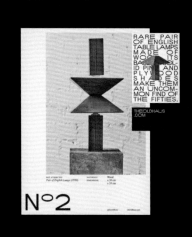

N°2

JOE
COLOM
BO

N°1

ALDO
VAN DEN
NIEUWE
LAAR

N°1

RUUD
JAN
KOKKE

N°2

FRANCO
ALBINI

N°2

THANK
YOU
THANK
YOU
THANK
YOU
THANK
YOU
THANK
YOU
THANK
YOU

OLDHAUS

JOE
COLOM
BO

4801
ARM
CHAIR
(1965)

THE JOE COLOMBO ARMCHAIR IS A SYMBOL OF DESIGN FROM THE SIXTIES AND HAS BEEN DISPLAYED INTERNATIONALLY AT THE MOMA IN NEW YORK AND THE CENTRE POMPIDOU IN PARIS. ORIGINALLY DESIGNED BY JOE COLOMBO IN 1965, IT WAS THE FIRST PIECE MADE ENTIRELY OF WOOD THAT KARTELL EVER PRODUCED. THIS 4801 ARMCHAIR IN TRANSPARENT CRYSTAL FINISH IS A REISSUE IN HIGH CLASS PLASTIC OF THE ORIGINAL DESIGN.

CINI
BOERI

ABAT
JOUR
LAMP
(1975)

OVERSIZED TABLE LAMP DESIGNED BY CINI BOERI FOR ARTELUCE. THIS PIECE OF ARCH WITH ARCHETYPAL SHAPE WAS EXHIBITED AT THE TRIENNALE DESIGN MUSEUM IN MILAN. ITS PYRAMIDAL MARBLE BASE SUPPORTS THE WHITE ACRYLIC SHADE WITH A BLACK METAL DIFFUSER (FOUR BULB FITTINGS).

ABC

MIES VAN
DER ROHE
(1886-1969)

ALVAR AALTO
(1898-1976)

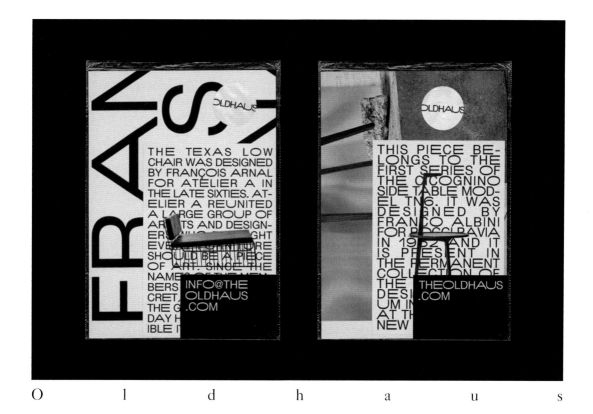

O   l   d   h   a   u   s

2018 — Visual Identity
Client: Oldhaus
Typeface: Oldhaus Regular (Naranjo-Etxeberria),
Times New Roman (Stanley Morison)
Design: Naranjo-Etxeberria

Oldhaus is a contemporary digital gallery specialising in limited and exclusive collections of art, design, and pottery. In developing the complete and cohesive visual language for the gallery's branding, stationery, typography, photography, and web, Naranjo-Etxeberria created an identity system featuring five values: uniqueness through the creation of a typeface, elegance through a classic secondary typeface, personality through the colour palette, sensitivity by the composition, and aspiration through the photographic language.

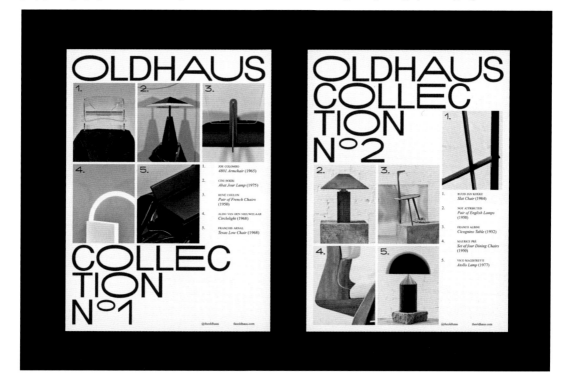

51st **Karlovy Vary** **International** **Film**

Festival

1–9 July 2016

52ND
KARLOVY VARY
INTERNATIONAL
FILM FESTIVAL
JUNE 30–
JULY 8, 2017

52ND
KARLOVY VARY
INTERNATIONAL
FILM FESTIVAL
JUNE 30–
JULY 8, 2017

52ND
KARLOVY VARY
INTERNATIONAL
FILM FESTIVAL
JUNE 30–
JULY 8, 2017

51st and 52nd Karlovy Vary IFF
2016, 17 — Poster
Client: Film Servis Festival Karlovy Vary
Typeface: Druk (Berton Hasebe, Commercial Type),
Helvetica Neue (Max Miedinger and Linotype Design Studio)
Design: Studio Najbrt

During years, KVIFF employed photographs of real and fictional festivalgoers for its visual identity, and the 2016 and 2017 editions continued to play with this concept of relationships between celebrities and normal people. Zuzana Lednická, Aleš Najbrt, Michal Nanoru, and photographer Václav Jirásek worked with covered faces in 2016, and followed up the next year with the dream of being a movie star, if only for a brief moment. While no one was recognisable in 2016 even with glam everywhere, in 2017, they mostly combined ordinary environments with iconic faces of both Czech and international cinema. "On the internet, nobody knows you're a dog," says an adage about virtual anonymity. "I is another," says Zuzana Lednická, but in reality, it was Arthur Rimbaud. "Malkovich, Malkovich, Malkovich ..." say John Malkovich's heads in John Malkovich's head to John Malkovich, who plays John Malkovich in Being John Malkovich. Everyone wants to be someone else. Everybody plays the theatre. And more and more roles, not only on Facebook and Instagram, but especially on the occasions that allow us to escape the everyday such as when going to the festival in Karlovy Vary. The identity game has never been easier (in this case, all you need is the consent of all of the portrayed stars!). Some want to be Belmondo or beautiful Jana Brejchová, some, these days unfortunately way too often, The Cremator. Famous actors in the movies borrow the identities of our infamous lives and give them the weight of their faces and bodies. We then project ourselves onto them. The actors play their lives in tabloids – actress Geislerová in bed with the festival's president! – and our lives in film, and we play at them. It comes full circle when Aña poses with the portrait of herself. Even Aña Geislerová sometimes wants to be Aña Geislerová.

BŒUFS 2017 JEU. 23 MARS
LA PÉNICHE CANCALE
VAPORETTO

BŒUFS 2017 MAR. 11 AVRIL
THÉÂTRE DE LA FONTAINE D'OUCHE
VAPORETTO

BŒUFS 2016 JEU. 22 SEPT.
LA PÉNICHE CANCALE
VAPORETTO

BŒUFS 2016 JEU. 1er DÉC.
St APOLLINAIRE
VAPORETTO

Bœufs Vaporetto
2015, 17 — Poster
Client: Association Vaporetto
Typeface: Custom, Work Sans (Wei Huang , Google Fonts)
Design: Atelier Tout va bien

Bœufs Vaporetto is a festive, musical hootenanny that happens in different places in Dijon. Whether it is jazzy, funky, or rock-oriented, each session is unique as a new amateur band is invited to play. Its visual identity system relies on a special lettering system that makes all nine letters in the word "Vaporetto" unique for every single flyer; all of which are RISO-printed by Atelier Tout va bien.

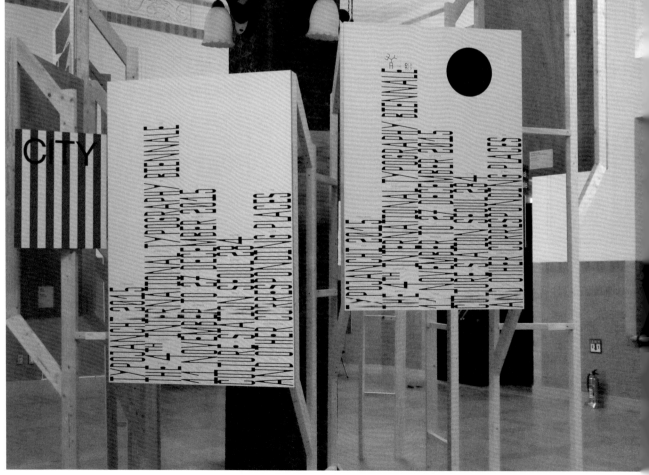

Typojanchi International
2017 — Visual Identity
Client: Typography Biennale

Typeface   :   Custom   (Helmo)

Design: Helmo
Curator: Jaemin Lee
Display Structure (Posters): Zero Lab

This visual identity system for Typography Bienanale 2017
allows for the composition of the same visual in different
proportions, from flag to poster, or banner to press ads.

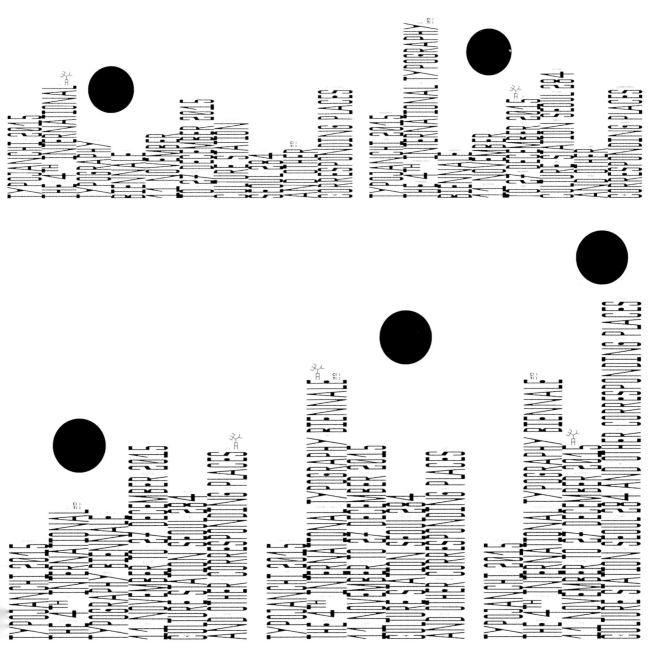

COMING SOON

LIGETI
STRAUSS
TSCHAIKOWSKY
PETRENKO
DAMRAU

BAYERISCHES STAATSORCHESTER

GYÖRGY LIGETI LONTANO · RICHARD STRAUSS VIER LETZTE LIEDER · PETER I. TSCHAIKOWSKY SYMPHONIE NR. 5

1. AKADEMIEKONZERT · KIRILL PETRENKO, DIANA DAMRAU · NATIONALTHEATER, 19. UND 20. SEPTEMBER 2016, 20 UHR · WWW.STAATSORCHESTER.DE

COMING SOON

NONO
HAYDN
STRAWINSKY
BERIO
ROSSINI
HANNIGAN

BAYERISCHES STAATSORCHESTER

LUIGI NONO DJAMILA BOUPACHA · JOSEPH HAYDN SYMPHONIE NR. 49 LA PASSIONE · IGOR STRAWINSKY ANNE TRULELOVE'S SONG AUS THE RAKE'S PROGRESS · LUCIANO BERIO SEQUENZA NR. 3 · IGOF STRAWINSKY PULCINELLA-SUITE · GIOACHINO ROSSINI OUVERTÜRE ZU LA SCALA DI SETA

2. AKADEMIEKONZERT · BARBARA HANNIGAN · NATIONALTHEATER, 24. UND 25. OKTOBER 2016, 20 UHR · WWW.STAATSORCHESTER.DE

COMING SOON

SCHUMANN
BARTÓK
DEBUSSY
HOLLIGER
EBERLE

BAYERISCHES STAATSORCHESTER

ROBERT SCHUMANN MANFRED-OUVERTÜRE · BÉLA BARTÓK VIOLINKONZERT NR. 1, RHAPSODIE NR. 1 FÜR VIOLINE UND ORCHESTER · CLAUDE DEBUSSY IMAGES

3. AKADEMIEKONZERT · HEINZ HOLLIGER, VERONIKA EBERLE · NATIONALTHEATER, 6. UND 6. DEZEMBER 2016, 20 UHR · WWW.STAATSORCHESTER.DE

COMING SOON

MEDTNER
RACHMANINOW
PETRENKO
HAMELIN

BAYERISCHES STAATSORCHESTER

NIKOLAI K. MEDTNER KLAVIERKONZERT NR. 2 · SERGEI W. RACHMANINOW SYMPHONISCHE TÄNZE

4. AKADEMIEKONZERT · KIRILL PETRENKO, MARC-ANDRÉ HAMELIN · NATIONALTHEATER, 20. UND 21. FEBRUAR 2017, 20 UHR · WWW.STAATSORCHESTER.DE

What follows (Orchestra)
2016, 17 — Visual Identity
Client: Bavarian State Opera
Typeface: Druk (Berton Hasebe,
Commercial Type)
Design: Bureau Borsche

These posters for the orchestra were part of the collateral for the Bavarian State
Opera's 2016-2017 season, themed "What follows". Inspired by "a state of not
knowing what's going to happen next, but having a sneaking suspicion that a single decision could change everything", a pure and straightforward typographic
solution was employed for its visual identity to reference movie introductions.

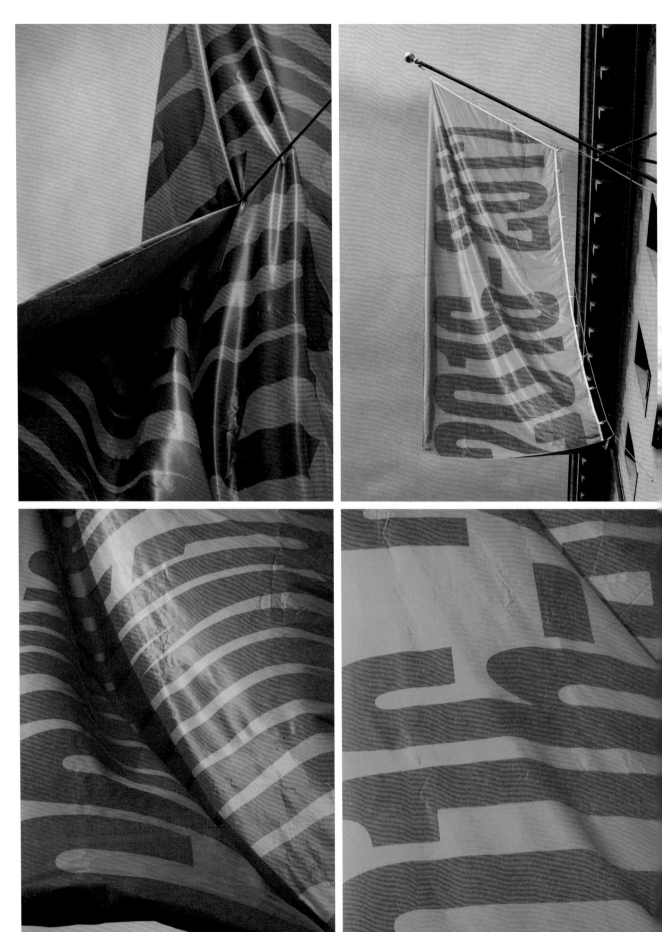

What   follows   (Opera)

2016, 17 — Flags
Client: Bavarian State Opera
Typeface: Druk (Berton Hasebe,
Commercial Type)
Design: Bureau Borsche

These striking flags were part of the communication materials for the Bavarian State Opera's 2016-2017 season, themed "What follows". Inspired by "a state of not knowing what's going to happen next, but having a sneaking suspicion that a single decision could change everything", one pure and straightforward typographic solution was employed for the flag text at the venue featuring vital information in succession, such as the theme, years, and "COMING SOON". A single square flag on the top of the building let passers-by read "yes" or "no", depending on their vantage point.

What follows (Festival)
2016, 17 — Flags
Client: Bavarian State Opera
Typeface: Druk (Berton Hasebe,
Commercial Type)

Design: Bureau   Borsche

These striking flags were part of the communication materials for the Bavarian State Opera's 2016-2017 season, themed "What follows". Inspired by "a state of not knowing what's going to happen next, but having a sneaking suspicion that a single decision could change everything", a pure and straightforward typographic solution was employed for the flag text at the festival venue featuring important details and the single word, "LIVE" for impact.

2 0 1 7 , 1 8 — V i s u a l I d e n t i t y

Client: Onassis Cultural Centre
Typeface: Various
Design: Beetroot Design Group

For their collaboration with the OCC, Beetroot Design Group were commissioned to design its 2017-2018 visual identity, including flyers, posters, programmes, and web banners in ways that would appeal to a large and diverse audience. In particular, they agreed to experiment with typography across those mediums to present all the season's events and, at the same time, communicate the OCC's identity and mission effectively.

"Flow Type", the specially designed typographic software, was developed by Beetroot Design Group to handle the large volume and diverse needs of the OCC's materials. It also played a huge part in the development of the season's visual identity. The typographic tool was created in the form of an Adobe InDesign script and an After Effects pseudo effect to help users approach typography in an expressive, restless, unexpected, and disruptive way. The tool also allows the concepts of motion and timeflow to express themselves, bending traditional typography rules. Flow Type gradually manipulates the values of every character in a text box in a linear or sinusoid fashion.

ATypI 2017
Montreal
12-16 Sept
Atypique

A17
Mtl

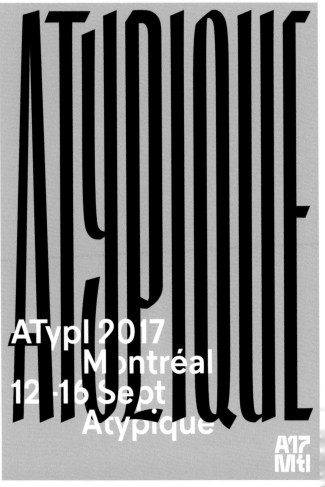

ATypI 2017
Montréal
12-16 Sept
Atypique

A17
Mtl

ATypI 2017
Montréal
12-16 Sept
Atypique

A17
Mtl

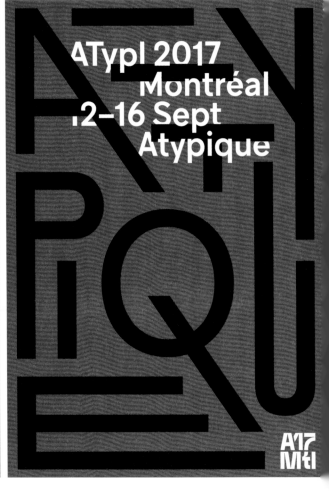

ATypI 2017
Montréal
12-16 Sept
Atypique

A17
Mtl

ATypI 2017
2017 — Visual Identity
Client: Association Typographique
Internationale (ATypI)

Typeface: Guillon (Feedtype),
Rozza (Denis Serebryakov),
Minotaur Beef (Jean-Baptiste Levée,
Production Type), Joe 182 (Jan Horĉík,
Heavyweight), Pareto (Erkin Karamemet,

Fabian Harb and Johannes Breyer, Dinamo),
Umbra (Robert Hunter Middleton),
Symptom, Octango, Sharp Grotesk
(Chantra Malee, Greg Gazdowicz, Lucas
Sharp, Octavio Pardo and Wei Huang,
Sharp Type), Grandur Alte, Frauen
(Lucas Sharp), Triade (Alexandre
Saumier Demers, Étienne Aubert
Bonn, Coppers and Brasses)
Design: Julien Hébert

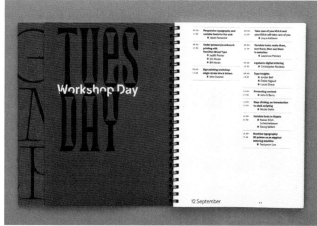

ATypI, or Association Typographique Internationale, is the largest organisation dedicated to typography. For 61 years, ATypI has brought together speakers and participants from around the world for five days of conferences and workshops. In 2017, the association chose Montreal as the host city and entrusted Julien Hébert to design its visual identity, as well as all the printed and digital materials for the event. The theme was "Atypique", French for atypical, and he sought to reflect in his work the concept of the city being full of dualities and contrasts: where East meets West, French meets English, old meets new.

JAZZ

26.7. DAVE HOLLAND PRISM   KENNY WERNER TRIO

27.7. JOSHUA REDMAN QUARTET   RED PLANET

28.7. JASON LINDNER   TOM HARRELL QUINTET

29.7. RALPH ALESSI BAIDA FEAT. GREG OSBY   MARIE KRUTTLI TRIO

30.7. JAMAL THOMAS BAND   BRECKER BROTHERS   THE JAZZ ORCHESTRA

JAZZ-NIGHTS.CH

NIGHTS

TÄGLICH AUF DEM VIEHMARKTS ALT LANGNAU: WORKSHOPKONZERTE AB 17.00   INTERNATIONAL JUNIOR JAZZ MEETING AB 19.00   ART AT LANGNAU JAZZ NIGHTS AB 18.00 IN DER ALTEN HALLE DER KUPFERSCHMIEDE LANGNAU MIT WERKEN VON MARTIN OTTH   LIVEKONZERTE AB 20.00 IN DER KUPFERSCHMIEDE, AUSSER 17.00 IN DER REFORMIERTEN KIRCHE

Langnau Jazz Nights

2 0 1 7 — P o s t e r

Client: Zurich University of the Arts
(for the Langnau Jazz Nights)
Typeface: Zurich Condensed /
Zurich Extended (Adrian Frutiger)
Design: Aurelia Peter

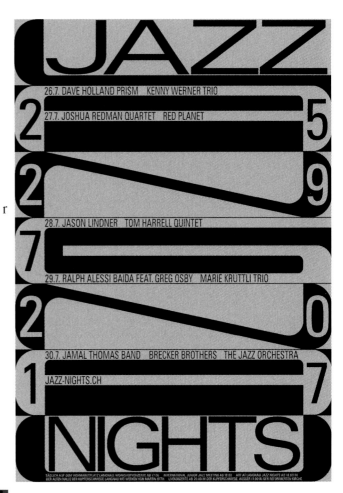

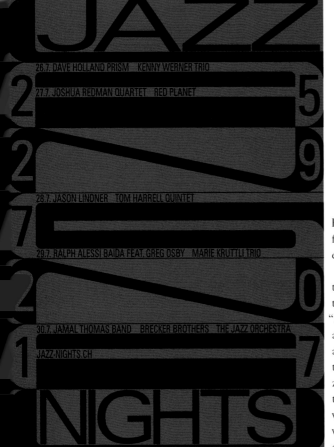

For Langnau Jazz Nights' poster design, Aurelia Peter focused on four central themes that she associated with the genre: rhythm, repetition, distorted notes, and spontaneous interactions.

The words "Jazz Nights" were placed in an extended style, with the rest of the information in a condensed style, to show the interaction between the distorted and short notes. The uppercase letters of "Langnau" were personally designed, with their format-filling width also reflecting distorted tones. The combination of the round and angular elements represented spontaneous interactions, whereas the rhythm and repetitions were made perceptible through the horizontal surface layout with its alternation between positive and negative colours, as well as through the concert information and dates which were placed in numbers from left to right. The three colour variations of the poster added presence and allowed additional interaction with the space surrounding them.

ACCELERATE OUT
OF
NOWHERE

PUNCHED

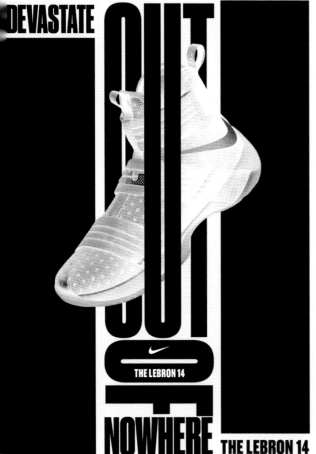

Accelerate Out of Nowhere
2015, 16 — Campaigns
Client: NIKE
Typeface: Various
Design: Bureau Borsche

Together with Nike's in-house agency based in Portland, USA, Bureau Borsche developed campaigns and supplied them with visual inspiration for their market worldwide, including graphics, logos, typefaces, colour and visual research as well as art direction. They explored all possible uses of campaign imagery and text to help Nike navigate and materialise the perfect outcome.

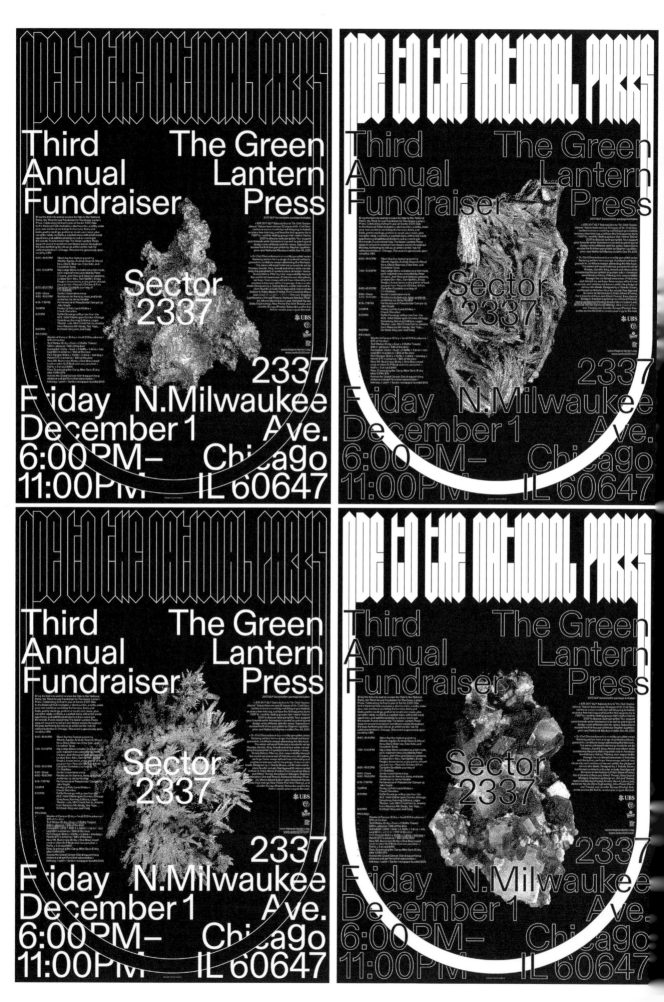

Ode To The National Parks
2017 — Poster
Client: The Green Lantern Press / Sector 2337
Typeface: Dia (Karl Gerstner and
Fabian Harb, Dinamo)

Design: Pouya A h m a d i

These posters were designed to celebrate Ode to the National Parks' fourth year at Sector 2337, an event that included a silent auction, a raffle, necklaces for humans, trees and birds, poetry readings, performance art, and music, plus campfire-ready cocktails, a curated menu with artist-made appetisers, and additional drinks to suit an evening in the woods. Funds raised helped The Green Lantern Press support non-commercial art and literary events throughout the year, furthering its role as an artist-centric hub for cultural activities in Chicago.

Lyrics!
2015 — Visual Identity
Client: Olivier Dermaux
Typeface: Explicit (Custom with Geff Pellet)

Design: B   u   i   l   d   i   n   g   Paris

Designed as part of an exhibition about music lyrics performed by contemporary artists and street artists, this book features the Explicit typeface.

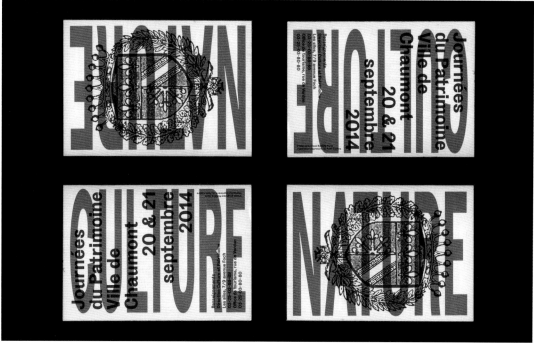

Journées du Patrimoine
2012, 13 — Visual Identity
Client: Ville de Chaumont
Typeface: La Fabrique (The Entente, Colophon)

Design: Building   P   a   r   i   s

These posters and leaflets were designed for "Heritage" in Chaumont, France.

In this project, Brando Corradini drew upon the artistic collaboration between the great Pablo Picasso and the "lighting innovator", Gjon Mili – a joint effort that highlighted how Picasso managed, in his genius, to paint not only using paint, but also with a strobe light. In turn, Mili's skills were demonstrated through his photography work that successfully captured the instantaneous light debris, which would otherwise have disappeared into darkness within seconds.

Les Freres Chapuisat,
Excrescence of Immortality
2015 — Publication

Client: Villa Merkel Esslingen
Typeface: Custom
Design: Bureau Progressiv

Bureau Progressiv's design for the exhibition Excrescence of Immortality by brothers Cyril and Gregory Chapuisat or Les Frères Chapuisat reflects the double-hinged purposes of the Villa Merkel's curatorial task. On one hand, the gallery discovers, reinforces, and conveys ideas to the public, while on the other, it acts as a competent partner to artists, as it moves towards fulfilling its goal of becoming more invested in artistic production. The work also corresponds with the Villa Merkel's self-image of representing younger positions in the contemporary art world.

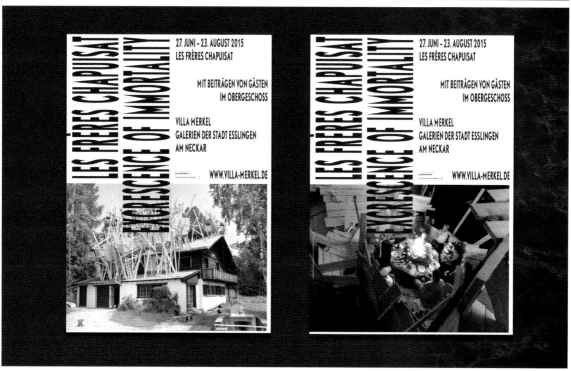

ABCDEFGHIJKL
MNOPQRST
UVWXYZ

abcdefghijklmnopq
rstuvwxyz

&0123456789

MMMMMMM
WVZNNNAA
RRCKKKOQ

ffrmMMNN

Love alternates

K K K

TRASH.

Zozoteur
animales & fil d'ariane

fold

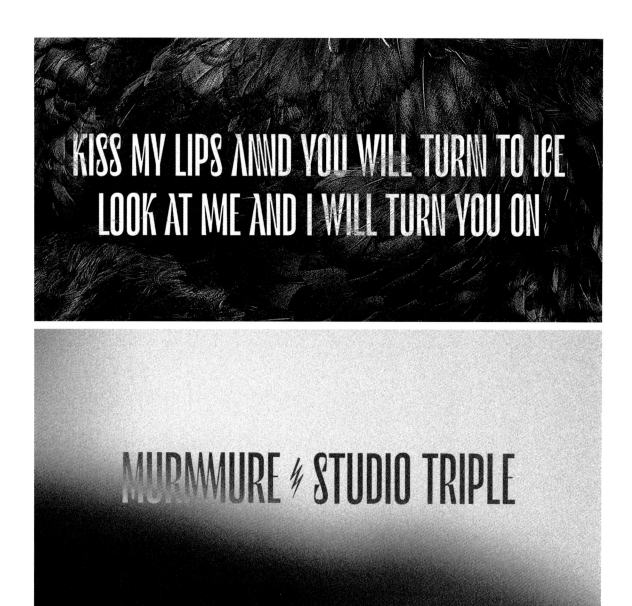

KISS MY LIPS ANND YOU WILL TURN TO ICE
LOOK AT ME AND I WILL TURN YOU ON

MURMMURE ⚡ STUDIO TRIPLE

Le Murmure
2018 — Typeface
Typeface: Le Murmure (Custom)

Design: Murmure

To renew their brand image, Murmure decided to focus on custom-designed typography, which resulted in the creation of the Murmure typeface ("Le Murmure" in French): an especially distinctive, editorial and elegant font that can be complemented by surprising stylistic variations. The studio developed it together with Jérémy Landes – a typographer at Studio Triple, a historical member of the Velvetyne Type Foundry, and the author of Solide Mirage – who lent an attentive ear throughout the process. Playing on a skilful mismatch between characters, Le Murmure creates a unique rhythm that reflects the brand's unique voice and image. This fruitful and enriching collaboration further strengthened Murmure's vision to undertake more singular and sensitive projects in the future.

NEO N.153 Refresh
2017 — Publication
Client: Ipsum

P
l
a
n
e
t

Typeface: Benton Sans
(Cyrus Highsmith
and David Berlow)
Design:
Naranjo-Etxeberria

Neo2 is an independent publication focused on creative culture.

Its new visual identity is based on the concept of changing numbers to reflect the constantly evolving nature of trends. While their tendencies are ephemeral, trends represent the present – which is why new graphic tendencies are added into every new issue. Previously, its identity was represented by a single typeface, but upon analysing past issues, Naranjo-Etxeberria found that this solution lacked personality and could induce typographical problems down the line. This resulted in the unifying of typographic styles to give the publication a sense of seamless cohesion.

Refix
2017 — Visual Identity
Client:

R

e

f

i

x

Typeface: Druk
(Berton Hasebe,
Commercial Type)
Design:
Naranjo-Etxeberria

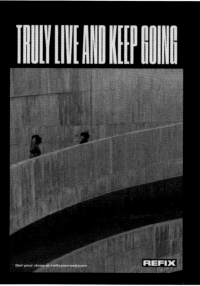

Likened to a breath of fresh air, Refix is a brand of water extracted from the Atlantic Ocean in Costa da Morte (Coast of Death) in Galicia, Spain.

Naranjo-Etxeberria were inspired by the fact that water is shapeless on its own, but always fits into the container that holds it. The brand's visual identity works the same way, with liquid adaptation being the core creative idea. Druk type was chosen as the main typeface because of the way its typographic family can expand and contract. That unique characteristic gave the studio the ability to adapt the identity across different mediums and formats –just like water does– with just a single typeface.

PLAYY

When you're playing in front of people, you gotta play your funky improvisation hard! Play it the loudest you can do & enjoy!

IT

LOUD!

Funk's Powerful
2014 — Poster Series
Client: Made at ECAL, Supervised by Diego Bontognali
Typeface: Bureau Grot (David Berlow)

Design: Nolan P a p a r e l l i

Inspired by his own drumming experience and the grooves of contemporary
funk tracks, Nolan Papparelli's pure typographical visual language results
in a strong visual impact. Each poster shows different types of information
about drums, ranging from technical notions to improvisational language.

PLENARSAAL
TYPOLABS
HOW FAR CAN WE GO

TYPO Labs Identity 2018
2017-18
Visual Identity, Typeface
Client: Monotype GmbH

Typeface: TYPO Labs Variable
(Bernd Volmer and Oliver Meier)
FF Attribute (Viktor Nübel)
Design: Bernd Volmer, Oliver Meier

The visual identity for TYPO Labs in 2018 is one of the first identities to use variable fonts as a key visual element. It features a bold custom-made typeface that was created by pushing type technology to its limits. "Variable fonts will make designers design in different ways. Instead of thinking about type being a range of static styles, they can think about it as something responsive, something animated and interactive, and something that fits all formats."

IED Visual Madrid
2015 — Poster
Client: IED Istituto Europeo di Design Madrid
Typeface: Compacta (Fred Lambert)
Design: Koln Studio

This artwork was created in 2015 to promote IED VISUAL, a design school in Madrid.

RIPOSTE

TECHNO
NEW WAVE
ELECTRONICA

25.03.17

QKC

PORTES: 23H
ENTRÉE: 5.–

VOX LOW
PARIS
SMBC
NEUCHÂTEL

WWW.CASE-A-CHOCS.CH

Design: De Roanoke

"RIPOSTE" is a bi-annual party in the QKC (Queen Kong Club) in Neuchâtel that showcases influential acts from the current techno scene. This poster was the first of a series for 2017, where the strong typographic composition of the word "RIPOSTE" stayed in a fixed position, and only information about the artists and dates needed updating for ease and cohesion. To accommodate low budgets, the posters were only printed in black and white, in limited quantities.

Rencontres Cinématographiques de Dijon
2016 — Visual Identity
Client: ARP, Ville de Dijon, ENSA Dijon
Typeface: Stratos (Yoann Minet, Production Type)
Design: Atelier Tout va bien

This visual identity is a nod to Étienne-Jules Marey, the French inventor and hero responsible for one of the most important cinematic legacies, chrono-photography, which captures movement in a single frame. Never fixed and always moving, the identity worked because of a three-lettered system put in place – resulting in a total of 2016 visual combinations made possible for all the printed matter.

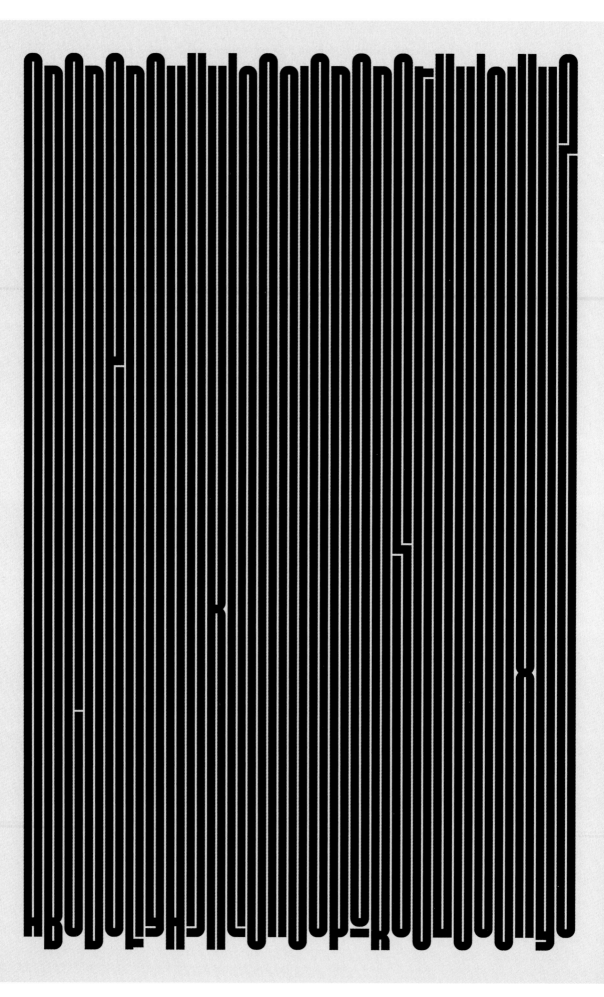

2014 — Type Specimen
Typeface: ITM Maas (Ivo Brouwer)
Design: Ivo Brouwer

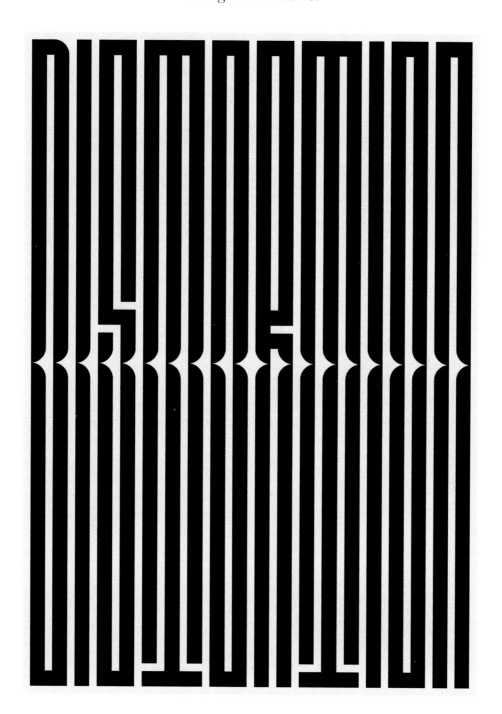

This type specimen is part of an experiment with modular
typography, where the height of the letters vary, but always
sticks to the same white space and tracking. Shapes within
the letters can change to either improve or worsen legibility,
and to aid or impede storytelling.

Coast Modern Exhibition
2014 — Exhibition
Client: Coast Modern/Twofold

Films/Mead Carney
Typeface: PP-Type 02 (Build)
Design: Build

This self-initiated poster is part of an on-going series titled "Word Power".

"Working with Nike is an extremely professional ping-pong process. The brand provides the emotion to be expressed and leaves it to the studio to manifest this emotion visually, allowing the team to explore and focus at their own will without worrying about a greater concept. For this reason, it is extremely refreshing and enjoyable." Over the last two years, Studio Feixen has had the pleasure to work for Nike Basketball on a variety of projects, including designing t-shirts for world stars such as Lebron James and Kevin Durant, as well as creating posters and typography concepts for Hyperdunk and the Bring your Game campaign.

The aim for this campaign was to create a design that conveyed the right feeling. "We played and messed around, we collaged, we cut and glued. It wasn't about big concepts, but all about uncovering a visual language that sported the same energy and excitement as a great basketball game."

RÉVOLUTION

ARCHITECTURE SOVIÉTIQUE

TYPOGRAPHIE CONSTRUCTION

MOSCOU U.R. REGULAR
UNE TYPOGRAPHIE
ENTRE UTOPIE ET RÉ

Le mouvement architectural né au
lendemain de la Révolution russe est un
cas particulier tant dans les concepts
développés que dans les formes produites.
Les propositions ces architectes des
années 1920 avaient pour but de changer
l'homme et son mode de vie.

Architecture Soviétique:
Typographie en Construction
2015 — Poster, Publication

Typeface: Moscou u.r. (C u s t o m)

Design: Bilal Sebei

The Soviétique architectural movement after the Russian Revolution is particular and unique due to the concepts developed, as well as the shapes and visuals produced. The propositions of the avant-garde architects from the 1920s reflect the notion of utopia and reality that characterises creation in the Soviet Union at the time. For this project that mixed photography and type design, Bilal Sebei decided to confront the image that he gleaned about the era from history books with reality. "By focusing on the Soviet Union's avant-garde buildings, the context in which they belonged to, as well as the heritage they left behind, I wanted to offer a personal look at the situation in the Russian capital after travelling to Moscow."

All of this was done as part of his graduation project at HEAD – Genève (Geneva School of Art and Design) in Visual Communication.

2013 — Visual Identity

Client: School of Design,
Hong Kong Polytechnic University

Design: Milkxhake

The 2013 Hong Kong PolyU Design Annual Show signified a new era for the PolyU School Design. Its theme "DESIGN MOVES." captured the excitement of the Core A block's relocation to a new space, exemplifying the way young talents move forward in their creative endeavours, as well as the vision for design to drive positive changes in people's lives.

The visual identity of the Annual Show went back to basics by using black and white for all publicity materials, reflecting a new beginning and a major milestone for the School of Design. The use of bold and customised typography echoed the fluid lines of the new architecture: the Jockey Club Innovation Tower designed by Zaha Hadid.

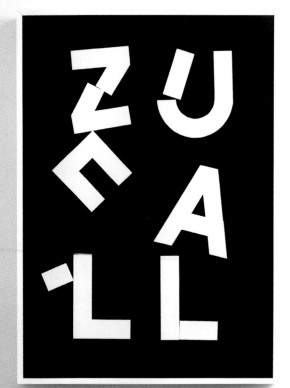

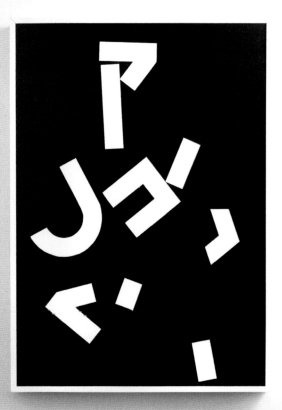

Design · Burrow

This poster installation was part of the Coincidence and Uncertainty thesis project at the University of Arts in Berlin in 2015. It was generated by a mechanical substructure, where internal machinery combined with external forces to lead to an endless self-generating, and ultimately unpredictable and incalculable stream of differing constellations as outcomes. By defragmenting the word "zufall" ("co-inci-dence" in English) into graphical elements and erratic rearrangements, each viewer was confronted with an abstract and dynamic depiction of the word itself. By presenting the characteristics of co-incidence in the form of uncertain results and the impossibility of replication, Burrow successfully brought its meaning to life.

The Gerrit Rietveld editorial project drew upon the artistic works of the great Dutch craftsman-designer of the same name in which two distinct personalities seem to emerge, making it hard to believe that his art was done by a single person. The first is that of the artisan cabinet maker, who reinvents chairs and furniture as if nobody had ever built them, following a very personal structural code. The second is that of the architect with elegant structures, committed to affirming European architecture through a rationalistic and neoplastic thesis. Corradini's design captures the unique way that these personalities alternate, overlap, and blend in perfect osmosis to create innovative and amazing works of art.

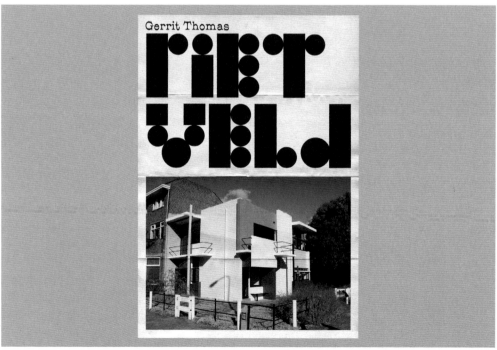

Together
2016 — Visual Identity
Client: Academy of Design
and Crafts HDK

Typeface:
No(n)-sense Regular
(Tor Weibull)
Design: Tor Weibull

The visual identity for the 2016 Together furniture exhibition featured a custom-made typeface called No(n)-sense Regular designed by Tor Weibull (based on different kind of furnitures). The exhibition displayed work made by students from the Academy of Arts and Crafts in Gothenburg (HDK), and could be viewed at Ventura Lambrate in Milan, Italy and the A-venue gallery in Gothenburg, Sweden.

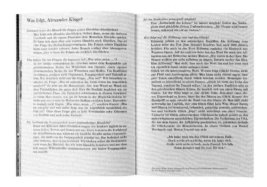

What follows (Opera)
2016, 17 — Season Guide
Client: Bavarian State Opera
Typeface: Various
Design: Bureau Borsche

In Nikolaus Bachler's words, the Bavarian State Opera's 2016-2017 theme "suggests just as much ending as new beginning. The question as to the consequences of our own actions in an ever more complex world leaves us all too often confused and provides the subject matter for our premieres".

Without a cover, this book has no beginning and no end. The open spine exposes its contents at first sight, leaving it vulnerable and revealed. Cracked open, it shows full-bleed imagery of film stills and cinematic references with matching typography.

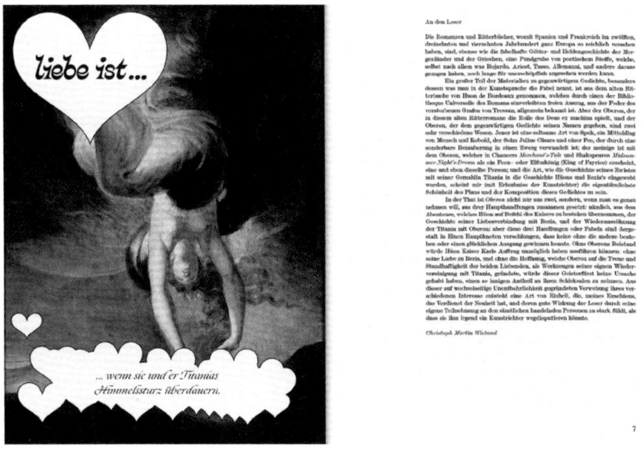

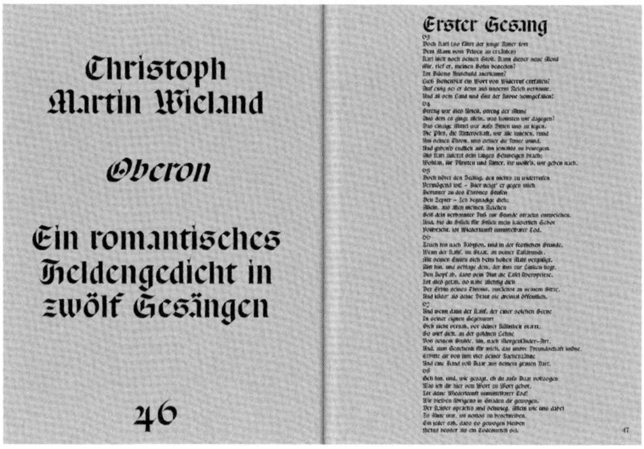

liebe ist...

... wenn sie und er Titanias Himmelssturz überdauern.

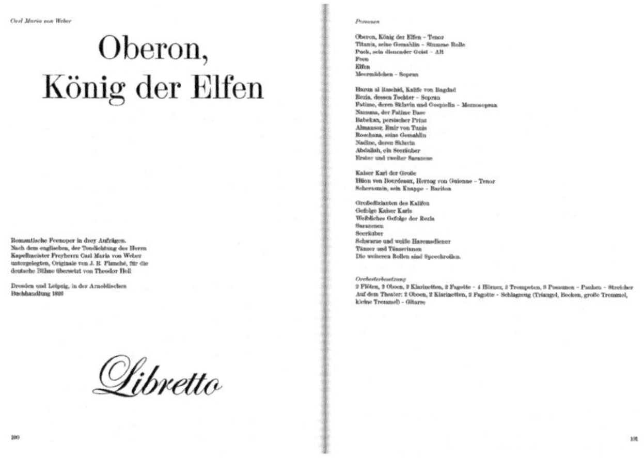

Sergej Liamin

Formen des Menschen-Möglichen

„Oberon" von Wieland bis Weber

20

PÖT, ABER MAXIMALE POESIE

EIN GESPRÄCH MIT DEM REGISSEUR UND PUPPENSPIELER NIKOLAUS HABJAN ÜBER SEIN METIER

50

Friedrich Schlegel

Gespräch über die Poesie

66

An den Leser

Die Romanzen und Ritterlieder, womit Spanien und Frankreich in zwölften, dreizehnten und vierzehnten Jahrhundert ganz Europa so reichlich versehen haben, sind, ebenso wie die fabelhafte Götter- und Heldengeschichte der Morgenländer und der Griechen, eine Fundgrube von poetischen Stoffen, welche, selber noch allem was Roberdo, Ariost, Tasso, Allemanni, und andere daraus gezogen haben, noch lange für unerschöpflich angesehen werden kann.

[body text continues, illegible]

Christoph Martin Wieland

Carl Maria von Weber

Oberon, König der Elfen

Romantische Feenoper in drei Aufzügen.
Nach dem englischen, der Dichtdichtung des Herrn Kapellmeister Freyherrn Carl Maria von Weber untergelegten, Originaltext von J. R. Planché, für die deutsche Bühne übersetzt von Theodor Hell.

Dresden und Leipzig, in der Arnoldischen Buchhandlung 1826

Libretto

Personen

Oberon, König der Elfen – Tenor
[cast list, illegible]

In dem Jahren 1827/28 beendet Johann Gottfried Gruber seine auf 40 Bände angewachsene Neue Ausgabe der Sämtlichen Werke von Christoph Martin Wieland mit einer ausführlichen Dichterbiographie, in deren abschließendem IX. Buch die Nachricht über die Uraufführung von Torquato Tasso auf dem Weimarer Hoftheater...

Ein romantisches Heldengedicht

Das Versepos Oberon, verfasst in den Jahren 1778/79, erscheint im Jahre 1780 im Teutschen Merkur...

Christoph Martin Wieland

Oberon

Ein romantisches Heldengedicht in zwölf Gesängen

46

Erster Gesang

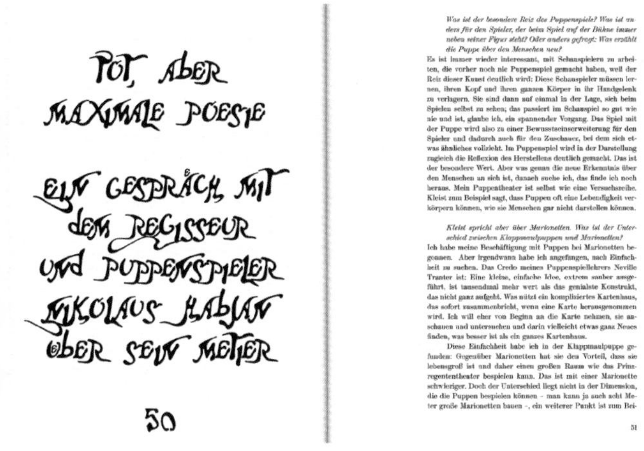

[poetry text, illegible]

Was ist der besondere Reiz des Puppenspiels? Was ist es denn für den Spieler, der beim Spiel auf der Bühne immer neben seiner Figur steht? Oder anders gefragt: Was erzählt die Puppe über den Menschen neu?

Es ist immer wieder interessant, mit Schauspielern zu arbeiten, die vorher noch nie Puppenspiel gemacht haben...

Oberon – König der Elfen
2016, 17 — Programme Book
Client: Bavarian State Opera
Typeface: Various
Design: Bureau Borsche

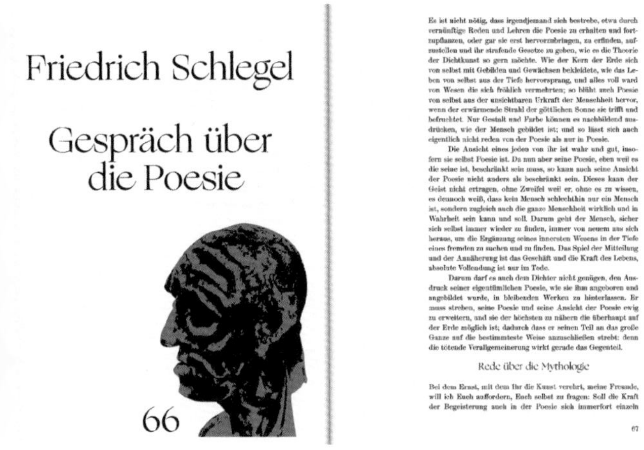

Es ist nicht nötig, dass irgendjemand sich bestrebe, etwa durch vernünftige Reden und Lehren die Poesie zu erhalten und fortzupflanzen...

liebe ist...

... wenn die Wüste zu blühen beginnt.

Ich ist, was nach allen Umbildungen noch die alte Natur und Kraft durchschimmern lässt, vor, die naive Tittime das Schein des Verkehrten und Verzüchteten...

UNDER THE INFLUENCE

OF

FASHION DESIGNER

DRIES VAN NOTEN

SPRING SUMMER 2017 COLLECTION

WORN BY

MANAMI KINOSHITA & LIZ ORD

AT STORM MANAGEMENT

PHOTOGRAPHED

BY

ADRIAN SAMSON

STYLED

BY

VANESSA COYLE

ON THE 14TH MARCH 2017, IN LONDON(UK)

& INTERVIEWED

BY

LEANNE WIERZBA

ON THE 22ND OF DECEMBER, 2016

HAIR BY	MAKEUP BY	MANICURE BY
ADAM SZABO	JANEEN WITHERSPOON	STEPHANIE STAUNTON

Hero Of My Own shot by Harry Carr & styled by Ondine Azoulay

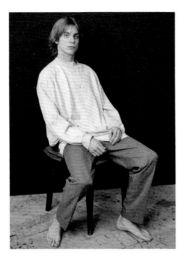

UNDER THE INFLUENCE

OF

PRODUCER AND
PERFORMER

EGON ELLIUT

REIMAGINING TECHNO AND
THE NEW TRUTH

IN CONVERSATION WITH
DAVID DORRELL

AND PHOTOGRAPHED BY
THOMAS HAUSER

AT THE PHOTOGRAPHER'S STUDIO IN BERLIN
ON FEBRUARY 18ᵀᴴ 2016

Under the Influence Magazine Design and Art Direction
2016, 17 — Magazine

Client: Under the Influence Magazine

Typeface: David (Émilie Rigaud, A is for Apple),
Shelley Script (Matthew Carter)
Design: VLF Studio

This art and design magazine was created in 2010.

Distraction, Seduction, Threat Direction by Arnaud Lajeunie and Georgia Pendlebury

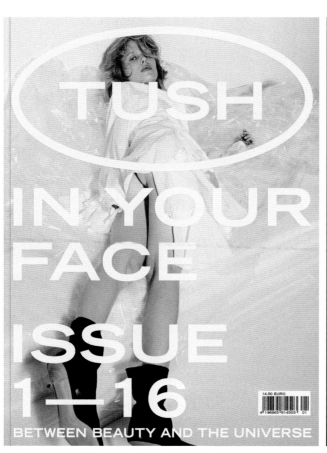

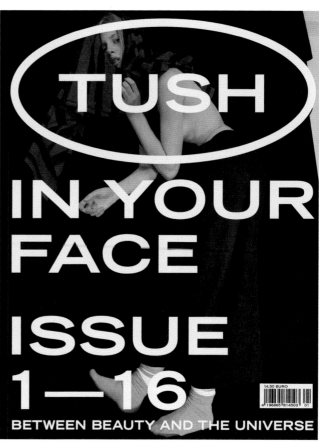

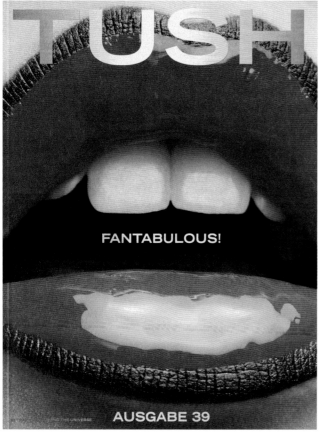

TUSH

PORTRAIT

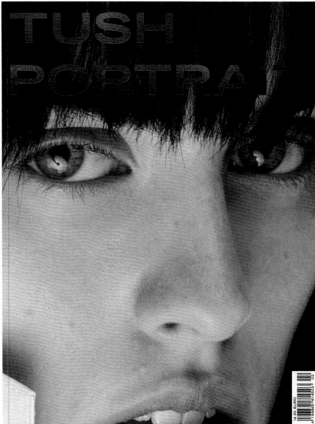

TUSH
PORTRAIT

Tush TenY ears
Forever Young
Issue 1 15

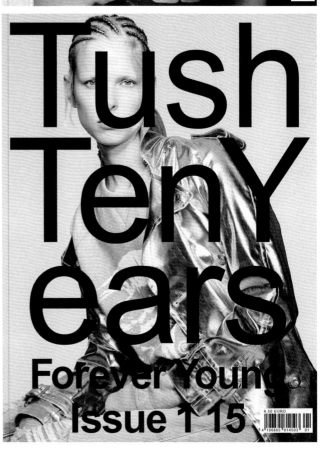

Tush TenY ears
Forever Young
Issue 1 15

INHALT

TUSH 1 16

Lip Color Rouge À Lèvres – 09 True Coral, 10 Cherry Lush, 15 Wild Ginger & 16 Scarlet Rouge TOM FORD

PORTRAIT DES ÉLÉMENTS ESSENTIELS

PHOTO
& PRODUCT
DESIGN BY
CYRIEL JACOB
REALISATION
& TEXT
NANE MEYER

Tush
N°2 2015

243

TEENAGE WILDLIFE
PAINT ARTIST
LEON
LÖWENTRAUT
FOTO
ARMIN MORBACH
REALISATION
LONI BAUR
264

2 PHOTO BY
MARIANNA
SANVITO

ORTRAIT
UNE FILLE
RBAINE

Foto OLIVER MARK
Realisation WIEBKE BREDEHORST & HEDI XANDT
78

FLOAT

Tush

Magazine
2012- 2016 — Magazine
Client: Armin Morbach
Typeface: Various
Design: Bureau Borsche

Founded in 2005 by German stylist and modern-day jet-setter Mr. Armin Morbach, Tush magazine is all about everything glamorous: fashion, beauty, design, art, and the latest of the latest. The Hamburg-based biannual is bursting with visual output and is an accurate gauge for up-and-coming creative starlets. Since 2012, Bureau Borsche has been in charge of its creative and art direction, making Tush an icon among magazine lovers. Continuous redesigns and experimental material solutions have become Tush's trademark and depict the magazine's ultra-en-vogue content.

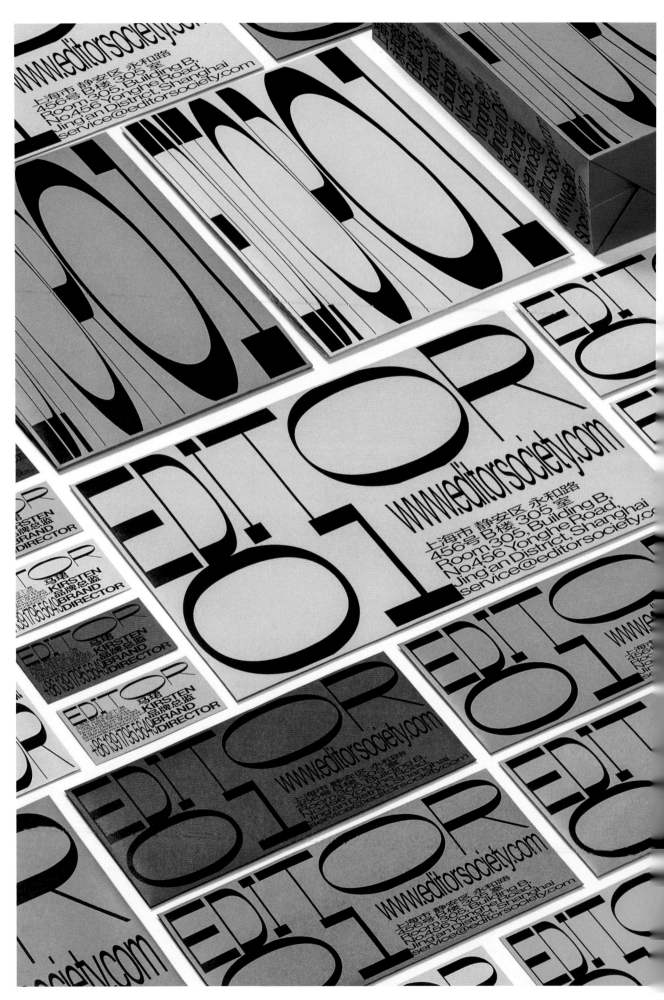

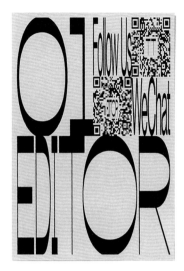

EDITOR
2017 — Visual Identity
Client: 边集 EDITOR
Typeface: Founder Lanting
(Li Qi, Founder Type),
Helvitica (Max Miedinger),
Custom

Design:

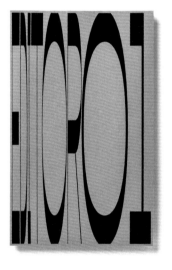

A Black

Cover

Design

EDITOR is a brand-new integrated business mode and has extremely high requirements for design expansibility, as well as the uniqueness of the design language. After several rounds of discussion, the studio found a design language that "almost no one had done before", which was prospective, easy-to-operate, and expandable. The concept drew upon the literal meaning of the word "editor" as a starting point, using an editor's thinking pattern where an image is a content space to be filled with information. This operation mode could cope with changes by sticking to a fundamental principle.

NA KIM
RED, YELLOW, BLUE
••••••••••••
OPENING NIGHT FRI
28.04.17 19 — 22H
EXHIBITION
29.04 — 30.09.17 √√
RIOT GHENT
#DDMSTWG 80

STIEN BEKAERT
TOUSE/TOUCHER
•••••••••••••••••••••
•••••••••••••••••••••
EXHIBITION SAT
01.07 16 — 20H
SUN 02.07 11 — 18H
RIOT GHENT
#DDMSTWG

BOOKSHOP ☺ ☺ ☺ ☺ ☺ ☺

ONLINE•••••••••••••••RIOT-GHENT.ORG

EDITIONS

RIOT-GHENT.ORG

RIOT
RIOT
RIOT
RIOT

ART X
BOOKS

dendermondsestwg 80, ghent
mon—fri, 10—18
sat 10—16
+32 9 223 39 53
info@riot-ghent.org

EXPERIMENTAL JETSET
WORD-THINGS IN
TIME-SPACE •••••••••••••••••
••••••••••••••••••••••
OPENING NIGHT THU
05.05.16 19 — 22H
EXHIBITION
06.05 — 24.09.16 ☹√√
RIOT GHENT
#DDMSTWG 80

Client: RIOT
Typeface: NTS (Josse Pyl), Swiss
Design: 6'56"

BIG JAMES

PIETERJAN GINCKELS
THU 29.09.16→16—22H

20 H
Record Release
APE#071
Pieterjan Ginckels
BUNSHAFT X PISTE

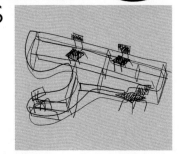

FRI 30.09.16→16—20H
SAT 01.10.16→16—20H

RIOT

RIOT is a gallery and bookshop in Ghent, initiated by the founders of Art Paper Editions (APE) focusing on new and emerging artists. Its visual identity was developed using the NTS font by Josse Pyl, who created "a new system in which the typesetter can set the letters both manually (with a grid and stencils) and digitally (with a keyboard). The system is based on the structural forms of our Latin alphabet. The typesetter doesn't work with letters, but with the components of the letters. By putting these in a certain position, the typesetter is free to shape his own signs and letters".

Client   :   *Felix*   *Bareis*

This artwork was proposed for the 3rd Jazz & Pop Festival organised by MHDK Stuttgart.

Client   :   Felix   Bareis

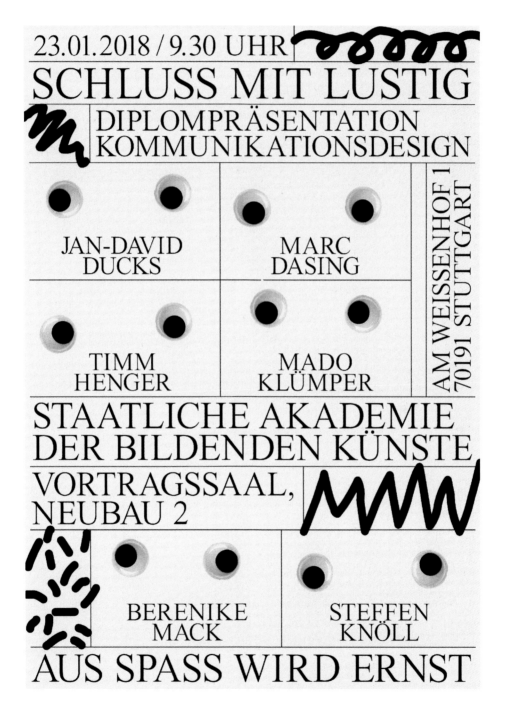

This poster announced the "end of leisurely living" through the use of real googly eyes.

entitled *Time is my Best Friend* written by Dorian van der Brempt was incorporated into the first STRT Kit publication. One could say in a day and age where time has become a commodity, as neoliberalisation manifests itself in the art world, the meaning of time has shifted: artistic time should be productive. The text advocates for a counter-development; to value slowness (a so-called luxury) and time for experimentation. The program tries to bridge this problem by providing artistic and financial support and allowing time for experimentation and in-depth research.

A crucial part of the program is a projectweek abroad... give the opportunity to meet artists and cultural producers from a specific area. For the 2016 edition opted for Athens, Documenta... projectweek The idea behind confronting them submerge... habits and con... that's not often seen is that of... different... the appropri... The appro... students with a presentation The work... who are given the... the real... artistic practice reti... the local context la... during the work... en... the presentation...

The year-long program... and cultural produc... visit the STRT Ki... ecting the visitors... ach artist's persona...

---

the visitors' program takes on a rather traditional approach, we also encourage residents to invite visitors on their own terms from diverse fields, which are not immediately linked to the arts.

STRT Kit is a program under constant development and self-reflection. We greatly value the partners, professionals and artists we work with. We are constantly reevaluating the program and carrying out our self-enforced ideology, trying new ways to extend our ideas and learning from our mistakes. In our work ethics we hope not only to provide support to the selected artists but also aim to create a sustainable community with all our partners, STRT Kit artists (from past and current editions) and the various professionals we work with. By doing so we value close and repetitive collaboration, we choose fair payment, and opt for the role of the student instead of the teacher when in communities foreign to us.

The publication

The first publication provided a response to an experimental year. Texts, images and interviews documented the process that the artists went through. More precisely, the publication operated as an archive from different perspectives: institutional, artistic, and theoretical. It also included contributions from our partners and narratives of loose encounters. These stories created a documentary overview of STRT Kit. For the second edition the publication takes another approach.

As the newly appointed coordinator...

---

perspective if needed. We decide[d] method focused on the artists' p[...] rather than the story of the insti[...] itself. This concept has become [...] twined with all of STRT Kit's a[...] including the present publicati[on].

To this end, the artists' involve[ment] was required so they were invit[ed to] co-think the content of the pub[...] and its format. We collectively [dis]cussed the purpose of a public[ation] in general: questioning collecti[ve] mitment, publications as artist[ic] professional tools, artistic state[...] archiving, etc.

These conversations resu[lted] in the decision that the public[ation] should consist of five sections. [Each] section zooms in on the indiv[idual] journey of each participant. Th[ey] worked closely with graphic d[esigner] Ines Cox, who was asked to cr[eate] unity between their individual [...] while also incorporating STRT[...] institutional program.

Each artist received a budget [...] a curator, thinker or scientist [...] a text about their work. These [...] have a double function, while [...] as the foundations of the pub[lication] they are to be used by the resi[...] a professional tool for the deve[lopment] of their artistic career. After b[eing] invited to think about the infl[uence] the program has had on their [...] practice, the artists worked pr[edom]inantly with images instead of [...] each creating a new work. On[e can] look upon these as five uniqu[e] editions. Finally, the publicati[on] wrapped in a plastic cover wh[...]

... Antwerp ... own artistic ... artists reacted to ... during the year. The ... contextualise the publica[tion] ... better understanding.

Introduction by Isabel Van Bos

This is an extension of Introduction by Greet Vlogels from the first STRT Kit publication.

Aside from providing much needed infrastructure and affordable workspaces for artists and creative entrepreneurs, Studio Start also envisions alternative ways of providing support to talented artists in order to sustain their careers. After multiple encounters and discussions with the tenants of the studios in their buildings, Studio... lowered their need for artistic... tense practice and oppor... up dialogues regarding

their work. STRT Kit, among other initiatives, was created as a response this necessity. Institutional collaborations, and offering young artists space time and depth to develop their artistic practice are the fundamentals of the program. The project is a co-production between AIR Antwerpen, Kunsthal Extra City Antwerp and H ART Magazine. While operating in a field where institutional collaborations might be seen as rare or risky rather than as an intelligent pooling of resources, Studio Start took up the opportunity to create a positive policy through sustainable collaborations. All institutions contribute and benefit mutually from their shared expertise and knowledge

STRT Kit   2016

The program

Five artists—Jim Campers, Ode de Kort, Maika Garnica, Timo van Grinsven and mountaincutter —worked in close collaboration with graphic designer Ines Cox to create this collective publication. It reflects on STRT Kit, an international development program for emerging visual artists based in Antwerp, initiated by Studio Start. Using their own artistic practice as a starting point, the artists reacted to the process they went through during the year. The following text aims to contextualise the publication, creating a tool for better understanding.

Introduction by Isabel Van Bos

This is an extension of Introduction by Greet Vlogels from the first STRT Kit publication.

Aside from providing much needed infrastructure and affordable workspaces for artists and creative entrepreneurs, Studio Start also envisions alternative ways of providing support to talented artists in order to sustain their careers. After multiple encounters and discussions with the tenants of the studios in their buildings, Studio Start discovered their need for artistic reflection, intense practice and opportunities to open up dialogues regarding

their work. STRT Kit, among other initiatives, was created as a response this necessity. Institutional collaborations, and offering young artists space time and depth to develop their artistic practice are the fundamentals of the program. The project is a co-production between AIR Antwerpen, Kunsthal Extra City Antwerp and H ART Magazine. While operating in a field where institutional collaborations might be seen as rare or risky rather than as an intelligent pooling of resources Studio Start took up the opportunity to create a positive policy through sustainable collaborations. All institutions contribute and benefit mutually from their shared expertise and knowledge

STRT Kit, a platform that provides support for visual artists working and/or living in Antwerp, invited Ines Cox to co-curate and design a publication to conclude its 2016 programme. They decided to focus on the artists' practice rather than the story of the institution itself: resulting in five individual publications instead of just one. This way, the artists could own a more personal document that functioned as a specific representation of their artistic practice. To create visual unity between the individual stories, Ines had to set up suitable parameters. Each publication had to be of the same size, and printed on the same paper using the same typeface – so that one could look upon them as five unique artist editions. The publications were then individually placed into plastic packaging that featured the institution's creds as well as text outlining the particular publication's aim. All five publications were then placed into a single plastic bag to physically keep everything together. When folded, the bag also acted like a cover with text that functioned as an introduction to all the five publications.

S T R T Kit 2016

2017 — Kit
Client: STRT Kit, initiated by Studio Start (Antwerp)
Typeface: Simoncini Garamond
(Francesco Simoncini and Claude Garamond)
Design: Ines Cox

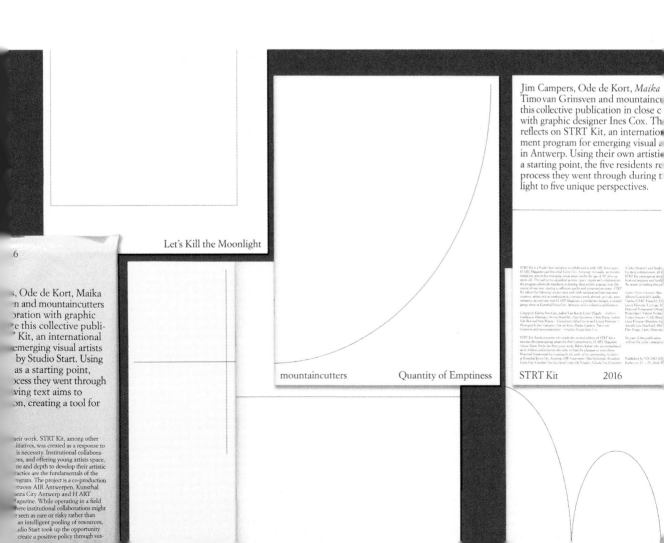

Let's Kill the Moonlight

mountaincutters   Quantity of Emptiness   STRT Kit   2016

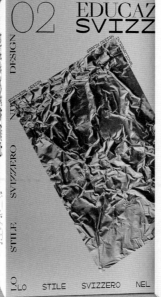
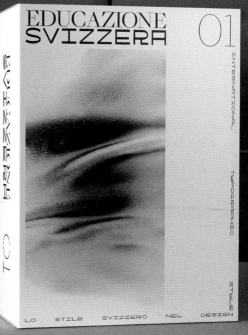

Educazione Svizzera
2017 — Visual Identity
Typeface: Various
Design: Brando Corradini

Brando Corradini sought to pay tribute to the graphic Swiss style that emphasises simplicity, harmony, visual pleasantness, readability, and above all, modernity – distinguishing it as the "International Typographic Style". The graphic work is minimal and represents the designer's own style, "less is more", where his entire creative philosophy is contained. In this editorial project, he featured the most important and representative works of graphic designer Muller Brockmann, which are still referenced as a source of inspiration for graphic designers all over the world today.

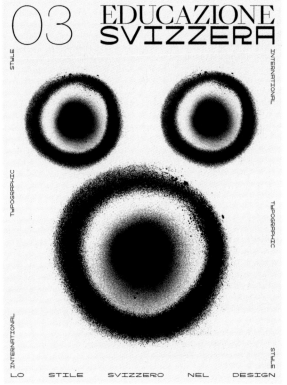

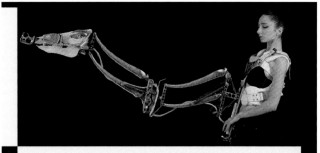

ZWANIKKEN FABRIEK
Christiaan Zwanikken
23 Februari — 30 April
Electriciteitsfabriek
Den Haag

ZWANIKKEN FABRIEK
24 februari – 30 april, 2017
Overzichtstentoonstelling
Christiaan Zwanikken
Electriciteitsfabriek, Den Haag

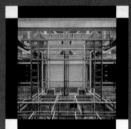

ELECTRICITEITS FABRIEK
podium voor kunstproducties in monumentale turbinehal

ELECTRICITEITS FABRIEK
ELECTRICITEITS FABRIEK
ELECTRICITEITS FABRIEK
ELECTRICITEITS FABRIEK

Client: Electriciteits Fabriek
Typeface: GZA (Mirco Schiavone and
Philipp Herrmann, Out of the Dark)
Design: Mainstudio / Edwin Van Gelder

Electriciteitsfabriek (EF) is a cultural centre in The Hague, located in a former office and factory built in the early 1900s. The centre's new systematic identity consists of street advertising, stationery, business cards, brochures, flyers, newsletters, and a new digital domain which reflects the cube-like architecture of the venue with exposed concrete and many structural I-beams. The site's user navigation system features contrasting bars of black and white that align with the domain's perimeter, and when clicked, triggers a seamless rotation of the background photo, which is of the actual venue. Users are literally shown the cube interior's facets as they explore the site, where information, for instance, is overlaid atop "photos" of space. This concept of organising information against the cube is seen in numerous ways (2D, 3D), extending to all aspects of this strong and cohesive visual identity.

Kafi Franz
2014 — Visual Identity
Client: Kafi Franz

Typeface: Etienne   (Tagir   Safayev)

Design: Bureau Collective

This visual identity was created for Kafi Franz in St.Gallen, Switzerland.
The restaurant and café invites diners into a world that fuses city flair and
living room charm to exude warm, uncomplicated, and home-made vibes.
Its name stands for fresh preparation and a creative seasonal cuisine, where
every month, a new "Franz" is featured for the Franz Dinner.

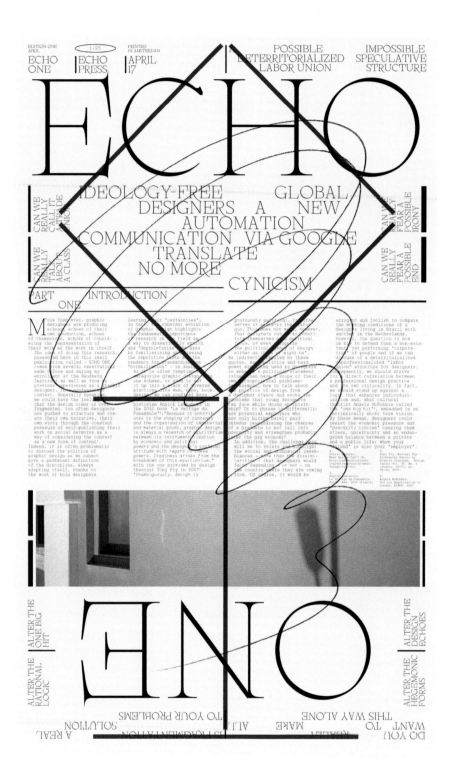

This poster/zine explores the possibility of building a trade union for graphic designers.

If You See Something,
Write Something
2018 — Poster
Client: Galerie für

Zeitgenössische Kunst Leipzig
Typeface: Canela
(Miguel Reyes, Commercial Type)
Design: Jim Kühnel

This poster was designed for a series of contemporary literature
events in Leipzig at GfZK (Galerie für Zeitgenössische Kunst).

KULTUR

Elektronika

Worldmusic

Rock

Hip Hop

FESTIVAL

Historisches und Völkerkundemuseum

WWW.KULTURFESTIVAL.CH

SG

Kulturfestival St.Gallen
2017 — Visual Identity
Client: Kulturfestival St. Gallen
Typeface: Pluton (Benoît Canaud), Atreju (Alyar Aynetchi),
Neue Haas Grotesk (Christian Schwartz)

Design: A u r e l i a   P e t e r

(with Laura Prim)

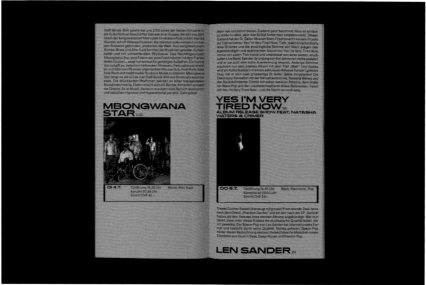

n collaboration with Laura Prim, Aurelia Peter developed and designed the visual identity for the 2017 Kulturfestival St.Gallen, a music festival in the courtyard of the Museum of History and Ethnology in Switzerland, that takes place in the summer. Its music programme usually varies from electronic music to world music to hip hop, with a line-up consisting of international stars and exciting artists from the region.

In their design, the four horizontal surfaces in which the numbers are placed are reminiscent of note lines, whereas the wide vertical lines on the side refer to bar lines, and the oval dots, to notes. Through closer inspection, a gradient dot pattern becomes visible, reminding the viewer of spotlights. The diversity of the music genres at the festival is shown through the interactions of the varying typefaces and their different weights.

KLASSEN:

Das Zeichen wird zur Arena des K.

Eröffnung
 20.07., 19 Uhr
Debatte (De / En)
 21.–22.07.
Magazin-Launch,
Debatte und Party
 16.09.

District Berlin
Bessemerstr. 2–14
12103 Berlin

Öffnungszeiten
 Mi–So, 14–18 Uhr

klassensprachen.org
district-berlin.com

21.07.–17.09.17
SPRACHEN:

Ausstellung,
Magazin, Debatte

mit
Kai Althoff/Isa Genzken
Gerry Bibby
Cana Bilir-Meier
Sean Bonney
Hans-Christian Dany
Övül Ö. Durmuşoğlu
Michaela Eichwald
Frank Engster
Fehras Publishing Practices
keyon gaskin
Sarah M. Harrison
Ann Hirsch
HATE MAGAZIN
Infofiction
Karl Holmqvist
Stephan Janitzky
Jutta Koether
Justin Lieberman
Hanne Lippard
Thomas Locher
Sidsel Meineche Hansen
Karolin Meunier
Rachel O'Reilly
Phase 2
Johannes Paul Raether
Monika Rinck
Aykan Safoğlu
Juliana Spahr
spot the silence
Starship
Jusef Olżau
Marlene Streeruwitz
Hans Stützer
Linda Stupart
Ryan Trecartin
Peter Wächtler
Ian White
Tanja Widmann
Frank B. Wilderson III
Susanne M. Winterling
Alenka Zupančić
und anderen

Klassensprachen wurde von Manuela Ammer,
Eva Birkenstock, Jenny Nachtigall,
Kerstin Stakemeier und Stephanie Weber initiiert
und ist ein Projekt von District Berlin.
Gefördert durch den Hauptstadtkulturfonds Berlin.

Ausstellungsdesign: Frank Lalande, Manspar
Grafik: Offshore Studio

HAUPT
STADT
KULTUR
FONDS

DISTRICT   jungle.world   cine

KUNSTVEREIN
FÜR DIE RHEINLANDE UND WESTFALEN
DÜSSELDORF

KLASSEN :

Eröffnung
    10.11.2017, 19:30 Uhr
Debatte, Performance
    11.11.2017, ab 14 Uhr
Workshop mit CAConrad
    18.–19.11.2017
Debatte
    20.01.2018, ab 14 Uhr

klassensprachen.org
kunstverein-duesseldorf.de

11.11. – 28.01.18

SPRACHEN :

Ausstellung,
Magazin, Debatte

mit
Kai Althoff/Isa Genzken
Gerry Bibby
Cana Bilir-Meier
CAConrad
Michaela Eichwald
Frank Engster
Fehras Publishing Practices
Sarah M. Harrison
Danny Hayward
Ann Hirsch
Karl Holmqvist
Infofiction
Stephan Janitzky
Jutta Koether
Justin Lieberman
Hanne Lippard
Thomas Locher
Karolin Meunier
Johannes Paul Raether
Aykan Safoğlu
spot the silence
Josef Strau
Hans Stützer
Linda Stupart
Ryan Trecartin
Marina Vishmidt
Peter Wächtler
Ian White
Tanja Widmann
und anderen

Klassensprachen wurde von Manuela Ammer,
Eva Birkenstock, Jenny Nachtigall,
Kerstin Stakemeier und Stephanie Weber initiiert.

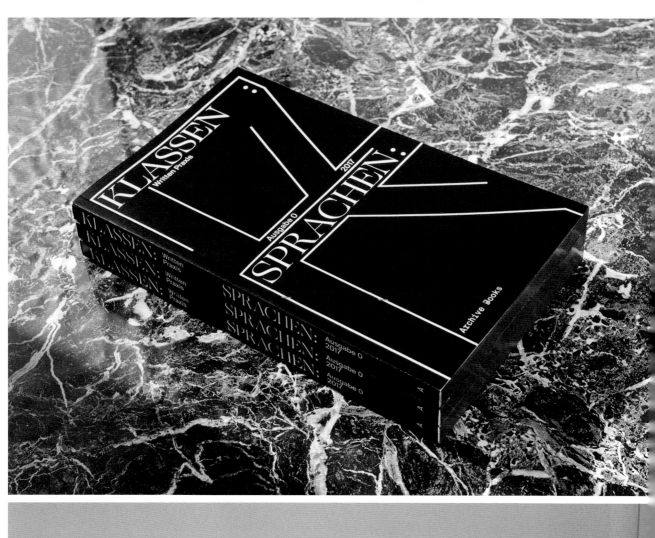
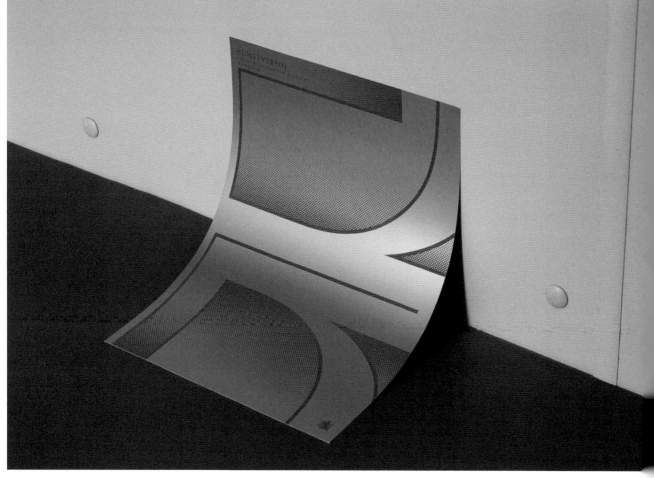

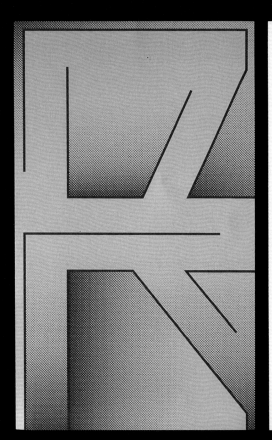

Klassensprachen

2017 — Visual Identity
Client: Manuela Ammer,
Eva Birkenstock, Jenny Nachtigall,
Kerstin Stakemeier and Stephanie Weber
Typeface: Suisse Int'l (Swiss Typefaces),
Ogg (Lucas Sharp and Greg Gazdowicz)
Design: Offshore Studio

The curatorial project Klassensprachen explores the interconnections of social class and language from an artistic perspective. Its visual identity features the letter "κ" in its centre – a letter that not only stands for the name of the project, but also the important concepts linked to it, like Capitalism (Kapitalismus), Communism (Kommunismus), Kafka or Commune (Kommune). Besides posters, invitations, and banners, a publication was also designed for the exhibition of the project, held in Berlin and Düsseldorf.

Tran

si

tio

nal

Speculation

2017 — Visual Identity
Client: Wang & Söderström
Typeface: True Terry (Custom)
Design: Tor Weibull

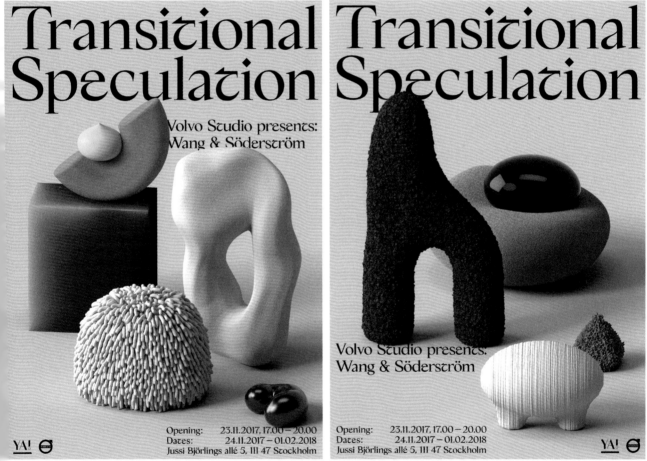

The visual identity for design duo Wang & Söderström's first solo exhibition entitled Transitional Speculation at Volvo Studio in Stockholm, Sweden, featured the custom-made typeface, True Terry, with two stylistic sets. It was used across a series of posters with unique exhibition graphics. Photography: © Beata Cervin and Wang & Söderström

BAYERISCHES STAATSBALLETT

SPIELZEIT 2016 – 2017

SPARTACUS, ALICE IM WUNDERLAND, GISELLE, ROMEO UND JULIA,
SINFONIE IN C, IN THE NIGHT, ADAM IS, LA BAYADÈRE,
EIN SOMMERNACHTSTRAUM, GALA MIT STARS DES STAATSBALLETTS,
BALLETTABEND - JUNGE CHOREOGRAPHEN, LA FILLE MAL GARDÉE

INFO / KARTEN
T 089 2185 1920
WWW.STAATSBALLETT.DE

BAYERISCHES STAATSBALLETT

GISELLE 23.09.16

CHOREOGRAPHIE PETER WRIGHT
MUSIK ADOLPHE ADAM
BÜHNE UND KOSTÜME PETER FARMER

INFO / KARTEN
T 089 2185 1920
WWW.STAATSBALLETT.DE

BAYERISCHES STAATSBALLETT

GISELLE 23.09.16

CHOREOGRAPHIE PETER WRIGHT
MUSIK ADOLPHE ADAM
BÜHNE UND KOSTÜME PETER FARMER

INFO / KARTEN
T 089 2185 1920
WWW.STAATSBALLETT.DE

BAYERISCHES STAATSBALLETT

LA FILLE MAL GARDEE 09.01.17

CHOREOGRAPHIE FREDERICK ASHTON
MUSIK FERDINAND HEROLD ARRANGIERT VON JOHN LANCHBERRY
BÜHNE UND KOSTÜME OSBERT LANCASTER

INFO / KARTEN
T 089 2185 1920
WWW.STAATSBALLETT.DE

2016, 17 — Visual Identity
Client: Bavarian State Opera
Typeface: Scotch Modern (Nick Shinn)
Design: Bureau Borsche

These posters were part of the collateral for the Bavarian State Opera's 2016-2017 season, themed "What follows". Inspired by "a state of not knowing what's going to happen next, but having a sneaking suspicion that a single decision could change everything", one pure and straightforward typographic solution was employed to reference movie introductions.

08pm—03pm
Blumenstrasse 15
Munich
Cash only!

THE HIGH

@the_high @the_high @the_high @the_high

LET'S KICK IT INTO HIGH GEAR! BLUMEN-STRASSE 15 MÜNCHEN DRINKOUR-BALLS.COM

@the_high @the_high @the_high @the_high

DON'T LEAVE ME HIGH AND DRY! BLUMEN-STRASSE 15 MÜNCHEN DRINKOUR-BALLS.COM

08pm—03pm
Blumenstrasse 15
Munich
Cash only!

THE HIGH

HIGHHI HIGHTHE

DROP BY AND GET HIGH

FANTASTIC HIGHBALLS

8PM TO 3AM

Blumenstrasse 15
80331 Munich

@thehigh_munich
drinkourballs.de

2016 — present
Client: The High
Typeface: High Times (AnyStudio),
Druk (Berton Hasebe, Commercial Type)
Design: Any Studio

The High is a bar serving contemporary high balls in the heart of Munich, where its interiors, drinks, and atmosphere could be described as a mix of the tropics and brutalism. With its combination of constrasting high-fidelity images and the sharp-edged yet flexible custom typeface, the visual identity aptly reflects the venue's aesthetic and exudes nostalgia.

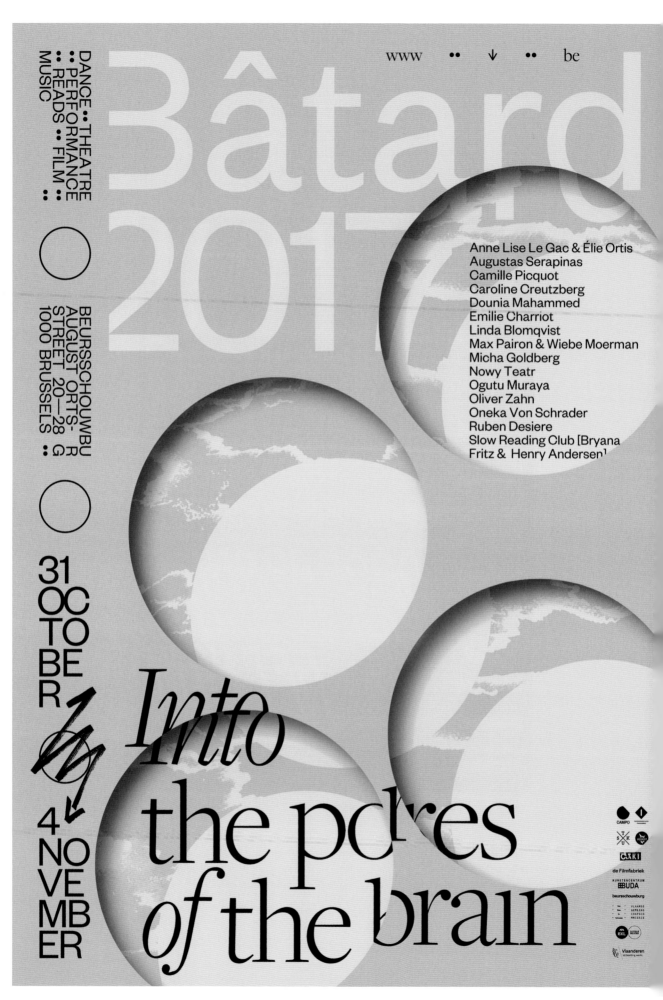

www •• ↓ •• be

Bâtard
2017

DANCE :: THEATRE :: PERFORMANCE :: READS :: FILM :: MUSIC ::

BEURSSCHOUWBU AUGUST ORTS- R STREET 20—28 G 1000 BRUSSELS ::

31 OCTOBER

4 NOVEMBER

Anne Lise Le Gac & Élie Ortis
Augustas Serapinas
Camille Picquot
Caroline Creutzberg
Dounia Mahammed
Emilie Charriot
Linda Blomqvist
Max Pairon & Wiebe Moerman
Micha Goldberg
Nowy Teatr
Ogutu Muraya
Oliver Zahn
Oneka Von Schrader
Ruben Desiere
Slow Reading Club [Bryana
Fritz & Henry Andersen]

Into the pores of the brain

CAMPO

de Filmfabriek
KUNSTENCENTRUM BUDA
beursschouwburg

Vlaanderen

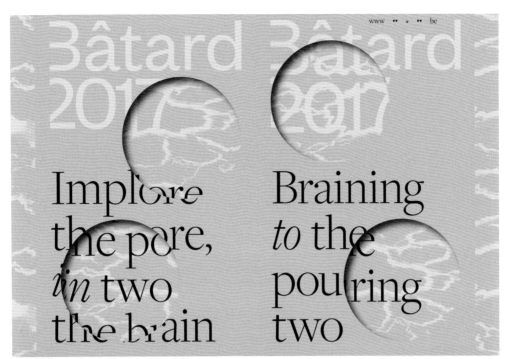

Bâtard Festival
2017 — Visual Identity
Client: Bâtard Festival, Beursschouwburg Brussels
Typeface: Founders Grotesk (Kris Sowers, Klim Type),
Freight Display (Joshua Darden)
Design: Ward Heirwegh

Once a year, Bâtard Festival takes over the Beursschouwburg in Brussels with a five-day programme filled with performances, theatre, dance, and film, where each year, a general theme is chosen to aid the curators with their selection. In 2017, "Into the pores of the brain" was its working title, and its visual identity mimicked the act of poring/pouring/bursting/moving. In some applications, brainwaves and holes were combined to create a flexible system that could adapt to the buzz of the festival.

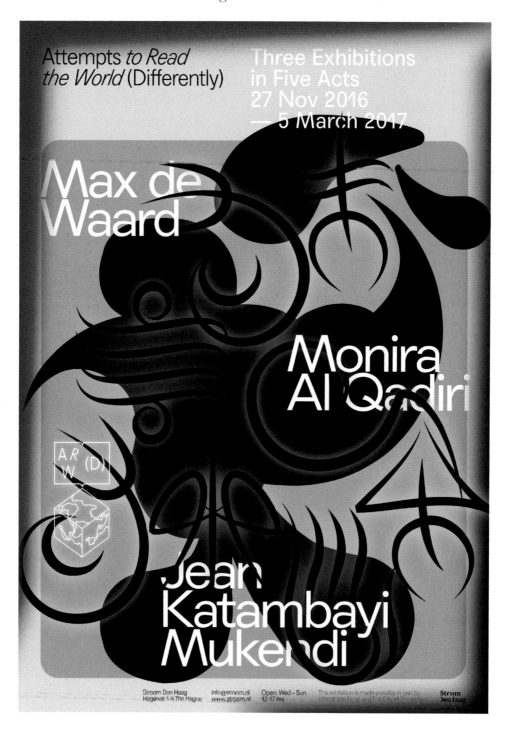

For the posters at Stroom Den Haag, the designers were inspired by their favourite action-fantasy game to translate the exhibiting artists' initials into runes. They also drew upon the concept of magic, with its power to transform, to breathe new life into the way people think about the ever-changing world – reflecting the artists' works. The outcome can be likened to magicians materialising alternative interpretations of reality through enchanting hand gestures.

How to Find True Love
and Happiness in the Present Day
2016 — Poster (DIN A1)
Client: Sebastian Nebe
Design: Lamm & Kirch

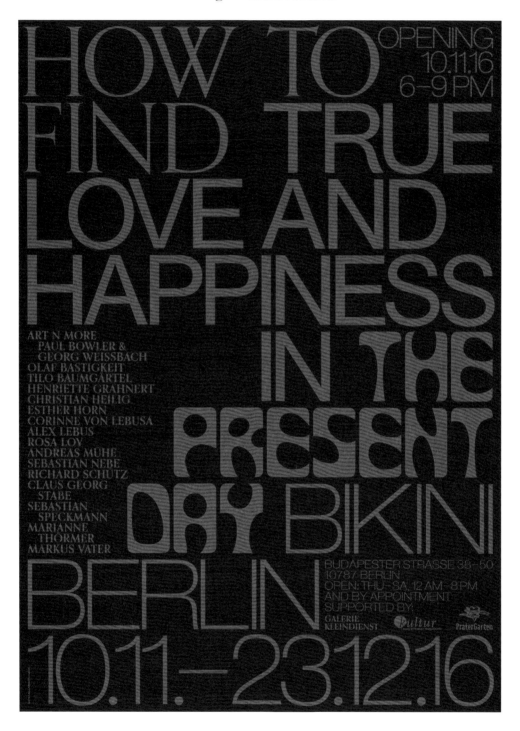

This poster was designed for an exhibition curated by Sebastian Nebe.

SAMMLUNG
THE NEUE
DIE
DESIGN
MUSEUM

GENTILLE
UNTITLED
AMERICAN
JEWELER
27.2. – 5.6.2016

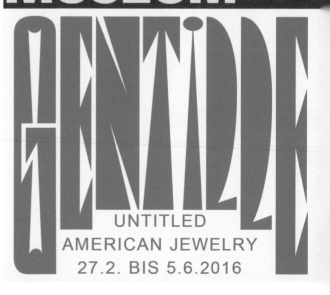

SAMMLUNG
THE NEUE
DIE
DESIGN
MUSEUM

MARCEL
BREUER

Die Neue Sammlung
2016 — Visual Identity
Client: The Design Museum

Typeface: Various
Design:
Bureau Borsche

Die Neue Sammlung is one of the leading design museums in the world. With over 100.000 catalogued items, it can lay claim to having one of the largest design collections displayed in a venue, with a wide selection of pieces ranging from the applied arts to industrial and graphic design. Founded in 1907, it is also the world's oldest design museum and one of four independent museums housed within the Pinakothek der Moderne in Munich, Germany. Its permanent exhibition showcases a selection of approximately 80.000 objects, and its featured shows on future-oriented design offer a varied playground of contemporary styles.

Bureau Borsche created the visual identity for Die Neue Sammlung using a basic flag as the main inspiration. The doubling of typography displayed the museum's name in both German and English, placed either horizontally or vertically to create a whole image.

The names of the designers featured in the museum were written in custom-made typefaces that aimed to emulate the core ideas of the designers' work without the need to show imagery. These typefaces offered a reduced yet fun form of creative freedom for the museum's poster designs, in-house lettering, advertisements, banners, flyers, and website design.

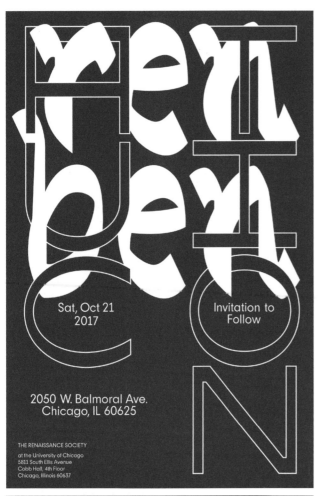

Sat, Oct 21
2017

Invitation to
Follow

2050 W. Balmoral Ave.
Chicago, IL 60625

THE RENAISSANCE SOCIETY
at the University of Chicago
5811 South Ellis Avenue
Cobb Hall, 4th Floor
Chicago, Illinois 60637

Ren Ben
2017

Gala and
Auction

Co-chaired by
Jorge Aguilar Cauz +
Ugo Alfano Casati
Richard Wright +
Valerie Carberry

Save
the Date

Ren Ben
2017

Ren Ben 2017 Gala and Auction
2017 — Visual Identity
Client: The Renaissance Society
Typeface: Fifty (Heejae Yang),
Penpals (George J. Acuna)
Design: Pouya Ahmadi

Artist-driven, ambitious, and always questioning: these are the values that make the Renaissance Society special. It offers artists a platform to explore new terrain, and builds a robust intellectual framework that responds to and expands on their work. The society's supporters also share this commitment to artists and their ideas, and in line with this philoso-phy, the yearly Ren Ben Gala and Auction brings together friends and members to raise a significant portion of its operating budget, which is essential to fulfilling their collective mission. This visual identity for the 2017 Ren Ben event explores the theme of contemporary Italian art.

2017 — Brand, Poster, Festival
Client: Struny podzimu
Typeface: Matter (Displaay)
Design: Studio Najbrt

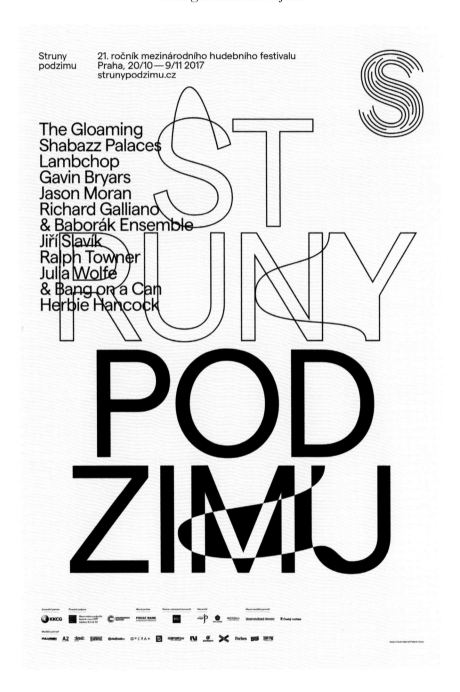

Back after a year-long pause, the Springs of Autumn multi-genre festival in Prague returned with a renewed team and visual identity in 2017. Martin Vácha designed an "s"-shaped logo from the word "Strings" and built upon the idea by "skipping a beat" in letter outlines from time to time, creating small glitches, dissonance, and experimental outcomes.

Am Alexanderplatz links
Klosterstraße 44 — 10179 Berlin
0049 (0)30 53 06 93 37 — hello@studio-laucke-siebein.com
www.studio-laucke-siebein.com
Montag—Freitag 9.00—18.00 Uhr
und nach Vereinbarung

GOOD
DESIGN
Curated
by
Johanna
Siebein

Eröffnung: 31. März — 18—21 Uhr

01.04. — 05.05.

Am Alexanderplatz links
Klosterstraße 44 — 10179 Berlin
0049 (0)30 53 06 93 37 — hello@studio-laucke-siebein.com
www.studio-laucke-siebein.com
Montag—Freitag 9.00—18.00 Uhr
und nach Vereinbarung

Neues
AIFABET
ISOSTAR

Eröffnung: 14. Mai 2010 — 18—21 Uhr

15.05. — 12.06.

Am Alexanderplatz links
Klosterstraße 44 — 10179 Berlin
0049 (0)30 53 06 93 37 — hello@studio-laucke-siebein.com
www.studio-laucke-siebein.com
Montag—Freitag 9.00—18.00 Uhr
und nach Vereinbarung

SCHÜ
LERZEI
TUNG
KLASSENFART
NACH
SCHLITZ

Eröffnung: 27. Februar 2010 — 18—21 Uhr

28.02. — 25.03.

Am Alexanderplatz links
Klosterstraße 44 — 10179 Berlin
0049 (0)30 53 06 93 37 — hello@studio-laucke-siebein.com
www.studio-laucke-siebein.com
Montag—Freitag 9.00—18.00 Uhr
und nach Vereinbarung

GOOD
DESIGN
Curated
by
Johanna
Siebein

Eröffnung: 31. März — 18—21 Uhr

01.04. — 05.05.

2010 — Visual Identity
Client: Id-Pure
Typeface: ZTF Idiot (Custom)
Design: Binger Laucke Siebein

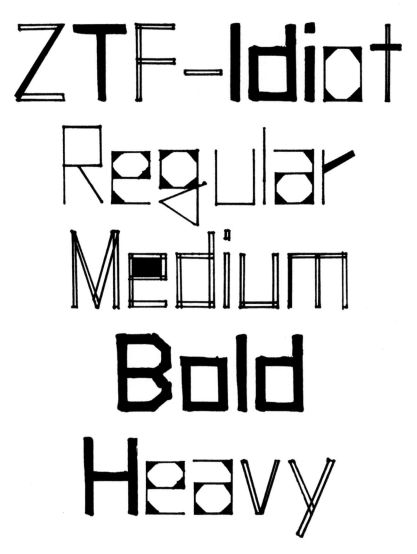

Studio Laucke Siebein for
Zeeburg Typefoundry

This typeface was created as the design studio's contribution to a special edition of Id-Pure, a Swiss design magazine, entitled "This is not Id-Pure". They were asked to deliver something that they thought of as "stupid" or rather, non-professional, which in their opinion was a "contradiction in terms". Invitations to a fake gallery were designed to reflect the awkwardness and charm of high school newspapers, when ambitious pupils try to keep things under control. The typeface itself was drawn as if only a ruler were available as a tool. Years later, the studio also used these designs in a series of colour cards for paint producer Akzo Nobel.

On

Move

ment

No.

I

2017 — Poster
Client: Francisco Regalado, Benjamin Skop
Typeface: Drescher Grotesk
(Arno Drescher and Nicolai Gogoll),
Custom
Design: Burrow

This series of silkscreen-printed announcement posters was made for the On Movement No. 1 exhibition by Francisco Regalado and Benjamin Skop. The two artists presented the viewer with interpretations of the deconstruction of movement by distorting the word "movement" itself. This was actualised by constantly shifting and tilting the silkscreen whilst printing different layers on paper. As such, the actual process of printing a poster became the main design element. Burrow worked with four different rotation angles, two screens, and four print runs each, generating a total of four poster variations. The customised black type was placed systematically by overlapping the previous layer, creating the illusion of sideway movements.

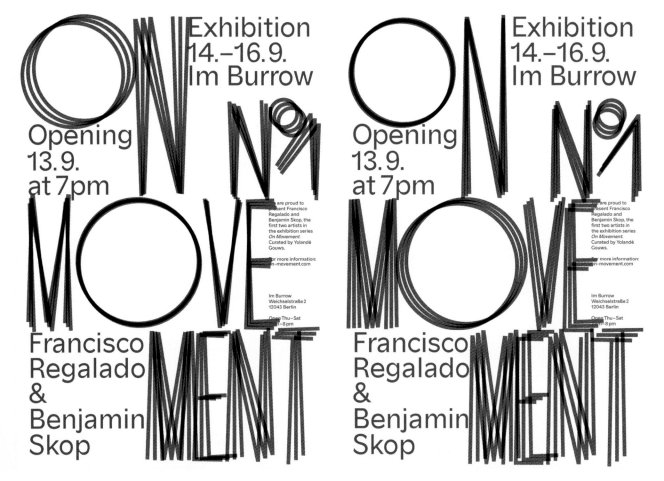

Client: Hochschule der Künste Bern
Typeface: Pano (Filip Matêjíĉek, Heavyweight)
Design: Offshore Studio

This poster was for designed for the art and design open day at the University of the Arts Bern.

Chess Instituut #3

Game Over

Bring your chess, get free beer.

Talks by:
Luc Vindaus
Anastasia Kubrak
Tom Kemp

Special guest:
Angela Jerardi

Sandberg Instituut,
Assembly Hall

Wed.
26th April
16–19h

2017 — Visual Identity
Client: Chess Instituut
Typeface: Jantra (Mateo Broillet), Handwriting
Design: Mateo Broillet

CHESS INSTITUUT at the Sandberg Instituut is a chess evening organised by students for students to enable the sharing of ideas between departments, and dialogues between artists and designers. This visual identity was made in collaboration with Tereza Ruller in 2017.

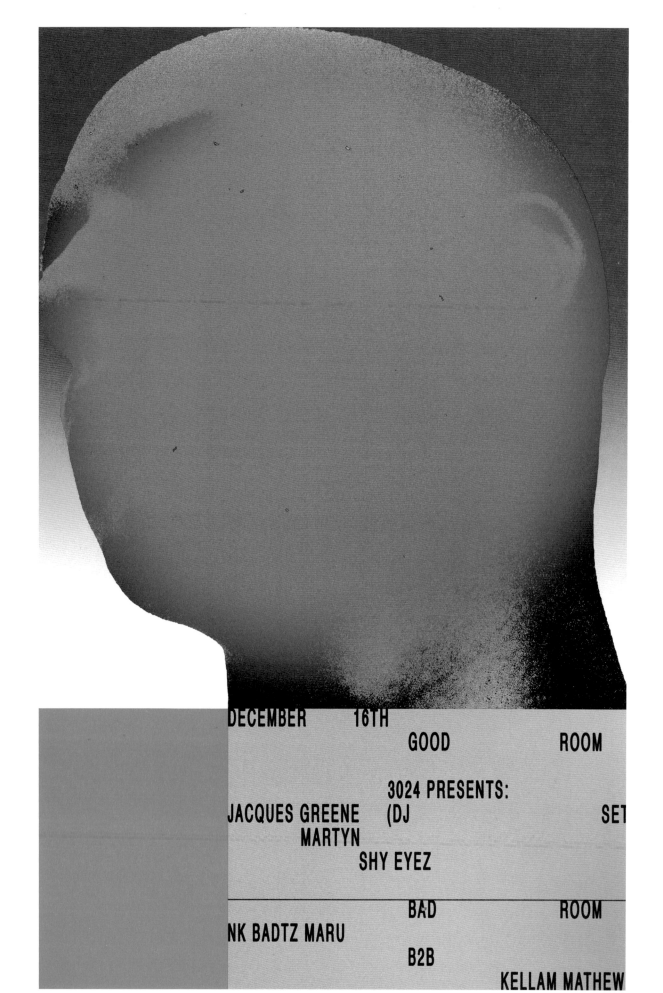

Good Room

2017, 18 — Posters
Client: Good Room
Typeface: Various

Design: Braulio Amado

These posters were designed for Good Room, an electronic music club in Brooklyn, NY.

April 20th 2018
Good Room - Frendzone!
Golden Donna (live)
Octo Octa
Kellam Matthews

Bad Room -
Remedy + Rhythmic Discourse:
Elena Colombi
Mscln
Amourette B2B Maroje T

JULY 8TH

GOOD RØOM

ARDALAN WORTHY

AKKI

GOOD ROOM

YAEJI

LOVE LETTERS

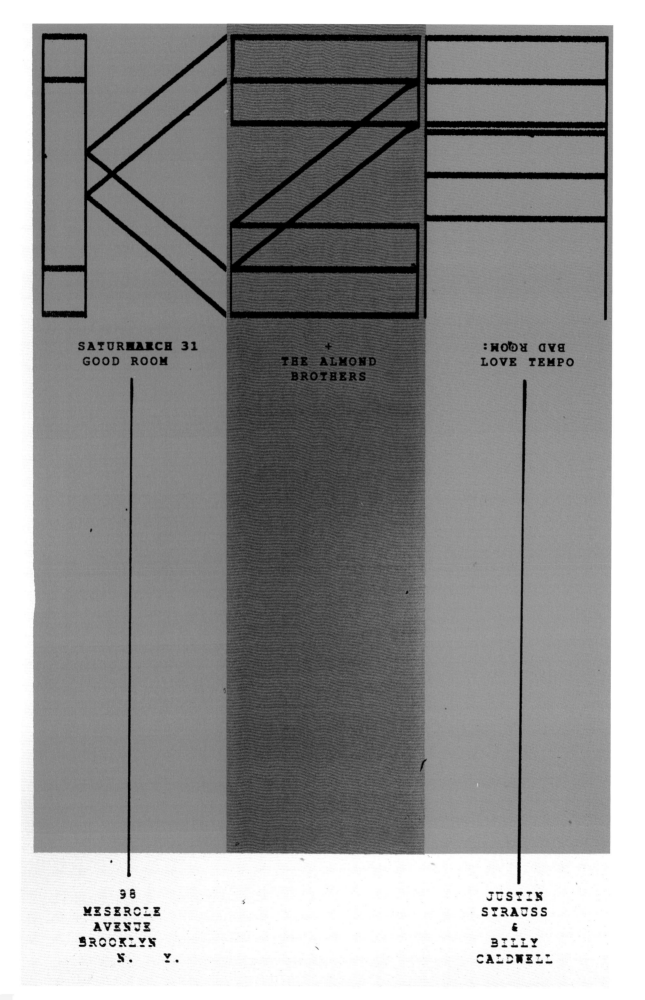

SATURMARCH 31
GOOD ROOM

+

THE ALMOND
BROTHERS

BAD ROOM:
LOVE TEMPO

98
MESEROLE
AVENUE
BROOKLYN
N. Y.

JUSTIN
STRAUSS
&
BILLY
CALDWELL

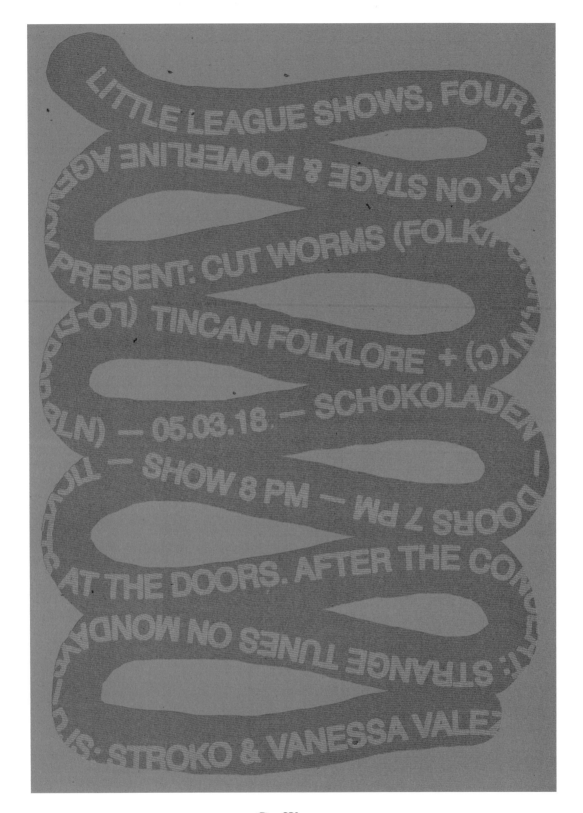

Cut Worms
2018 — Poster
Client: Little League Shows
Typeface : Helvetica (Max Miedinger)
Design : Braulio Amado

This poster was designed for the Cut Worms show in Berlin.

Im Schtei Poster Series
2015 — Poster
Client: Konzertkeller im Schtei, Sempach
Typeface : Custom
Design : Erich Brechbühl

This typographic poster was designed in 2015 for an "im Schtei" concert in Sempach, Switzerland.

MoMA PS1 Warm Up
MoMA PS1 Warm Up

MoMA PS1 Warm Up

MoMA PS1 Warm Up

2017 — Poster
Client: MoMA PS1
Typeface: PT Serif (Alexandra Korolkova,
Olga Umpeleva and Vladimir Yefimov, ParaType),
Sporting Grotesque (Lucas Le Bihan)
Design: Artem Matyushkin

MoMA PS1 Warm Up is a weekly outdoor live music series that presents the best in local and global electronic music across a range of genres. The content of this poster, which carries information on each week's events, can be presented as a whole, or modified according to the appropriate party and line-up using duct tape or the museum's stickers.

YOU LAUGH / 18.1.14

chhochschule Düss...dorf, Fachbereich Design inszeni... Humor als ästhetisch-m...n Komplem...
nce von Weiss...sten (Düsseldorf) ...laug... augh f...et im Ra...stin...schau...e B...hne. Design wird Performanc...

dorf & Sch...n des Amateurs, Grabb...g 4, 40221 Düs...ldorf/Vorträge und Dialog: Dr. Rainer Stollma...(Uni-
Stadtsparka...Düssel...Kunst- und Kultu...Kunst- und Kultur- und Sozialstiftung Provin...
Phne. Design wird Performanc.../18 Januar 201... 16:00 UhrKunsthalle...ssel...
...NE: Das Fest! statt. Mit...eundlic...stützu...der...shall...

You Laugh an Ugly Laugh
2013 — Campaign
Client: Practical assignment for Peter Behrens School of Arts
Typeface: Brush Script (Robert E. Smith, Adobe)
Design:

These designs were made for You Laugh an Ugly Laugh,
a performative exhibition and panel discussion on art and
humour in a temporary and social context during the Kun-
sthalle BÜHNE: Das Fest! in Düsseldorf.

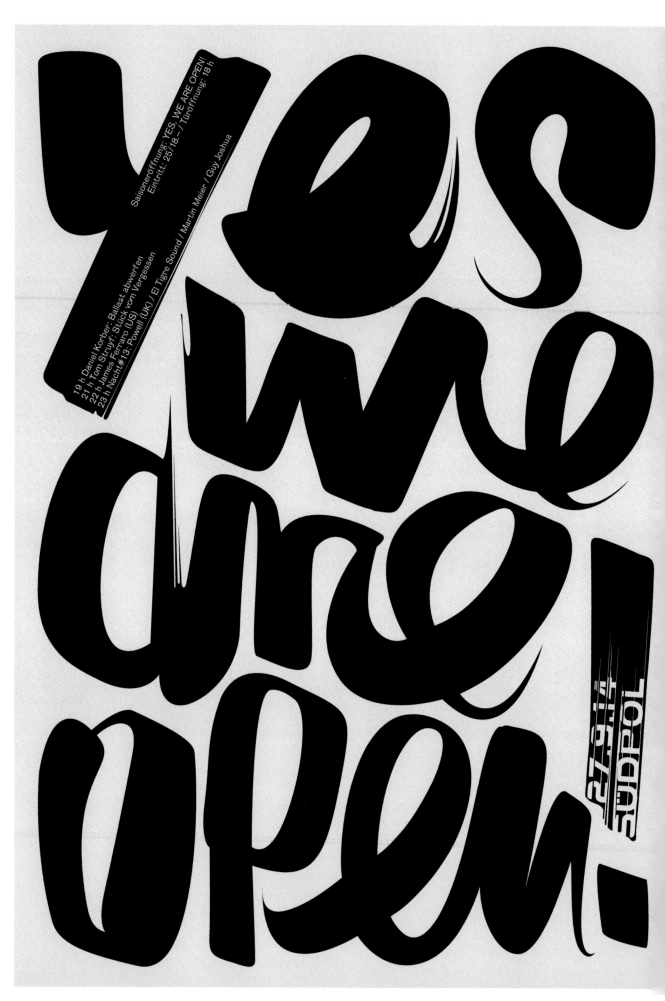

YES WE ARE OPEN.

Saisoneröffnung: YES, WE ARE OPEN!
Eintritt: 25/18.– / Türöffnung: 18 h

19 h Daniel Korber: Ballast abwerfen
21 h Tom Stryuf: Stück vom Vergessen
22 h James Ferraro (US) / El Tigre Sound / Martin Meier / Guy Joshua
23 h Nacht#13: Powell (UK) / El Tigre Sound / Martin Meier / Guy Joshua

27.9.14
SÜDPOL

2010-2015 — Poster
Client: Südpol
Typeface: Custom
Design: Studio Feixen

The Südpol is a multi-purpose cultural centre in Kriens, Switzerland. Besides housing a theatre, a symphony orchestra, a brass band, a music school, a restaurant, and a flea market, it also rents out space for performances of music, dance, theatre, literature, digital arts and many more. From 2010 to 2015, Felix Pfäffli was commissioned to design all the posters for the venue. With only marginal corporate design restrictions in place, a collaboration emerged over the years that allowed for design to cross the usual boundaries.

All these 42 cm x 30 cm posters were printed using the Risograph technique – a small-scale silkscreen print.

Conan Mockasin NZ
Konzert: Psy-Pop
Tür 20 h / Beginn 21 h
Eintritt:
25.-/18.-

9.1.15

Club: Konzert
Eintritt: 20 / 15.–

Tür: 21h
Begin: 22 h

Doomenfels &
Wavering Hands

SÜDPOL

Sucha Ort Plattentaufe ·Invisible· Support: Lipka
Club: Plattentaufe, Fest
Eintritt: 20 / 15.– | Tür: 21 h | Begin: 22 h

SÜDPOL

7.3.14

SÜDPOL

24.9.13

SÜDPOL

Au Revoir Simone (US) | Konzert: Pop
Eintritt: Fr. 25.– / 18.– | Tür: 20h | Begin: 21h

Welcome to Paradise
2016 — Poster
Client:
Sonah Theater Produktionen
Typeface: Custom
Design: Erich Brechbühl

These posters were made for a play about two immortal ladies who meet every year for their birthdays.

Open Club Day
2017 — Poster
Client: Neubad
Typeface: Unica Haas
(André Gürtler, Christian Mengelt, Erich Gschwind and Toshi Omagari)
Design: Erich Brechbühl

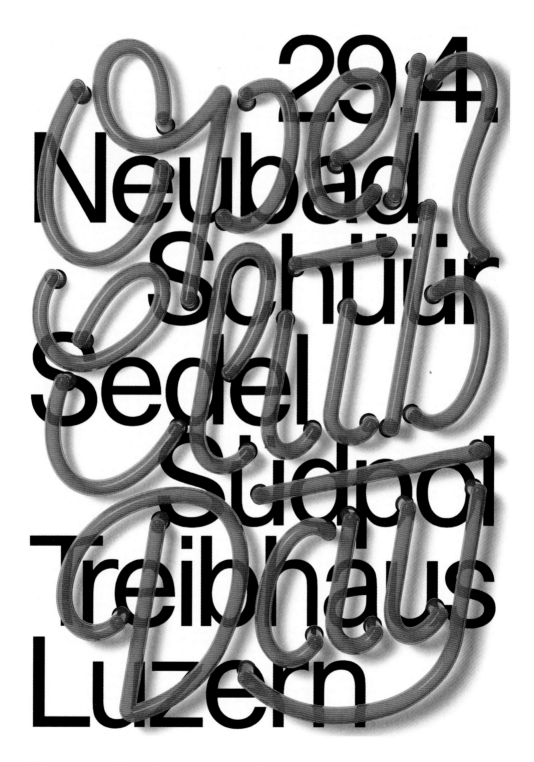

This poster was designed for the open house of five clubs in Lucerne, Switzerland in the daytime.

TAGE DER OFFENEN KULTUR

→ 23. 2017

21.– JULI

UNIVERSITÄT DER KÜNSTE BERLIN

Universität der Künste Berlin

KULTURradio rbb 92,4   TAGESSPIEGEL

Rundgang 2017
2013 — Poster
Client: University of the Arts Berlin
Typeface: GT America Expanded
(Noël Leu with Seb McLauchlan, Grilli Type)
Design: Denis Yilmaz

"Rundgang" is the University of the Arts Berlin's three-day annual open-day event – a festive gathering of students as well as people interested in the disciplines of fine arts, design, music, and more. This poster was proposed for the year 2017, where the balloons could be printed as an optional "golden" layer and the typographic elements could be used alone. An animated version showed the festive rise of the balloons within the physical dimensions of the poster itself.

Design: Studio Feixen

This poster was designed for Hermès perfumes' 2018
Christmas campaign, featuring a small set of patterns
with three main actors: Bubble, Bling, and Pong.

Design: Studio   Feixen

MIT Technology Review is a magazine published by the Massachusetts Institute of Technology. It was originally published in 1899 as a magazine for its own graduates, but the relaunch of the magazine in 1998 led to an unprecedented success. Within a very short time, the shelf-life of the magazine tripled, and today, there are editions of the Technology Review in China, Germany, and Italy. From time to time, Studio Feixen are asked to design a cover and for the Business Issue in 2015, they could not decide on a single option and ended up with two of their proposals printed. One was very technical in nature, playing with typography and statistics (this page), while the other one expanded upon the idea of a previous cover with a cursor flying into space.

Laboratorium
Wagenburgstr.140

24.09 / 20 Uhr

LIEBER
LEBEN
OSTEN
LASSEN

Mit   St. Tropez   Antiheld Singer-   Arcon Ultra
Ben Jakob   Songwriter-Set   Simon Jonas

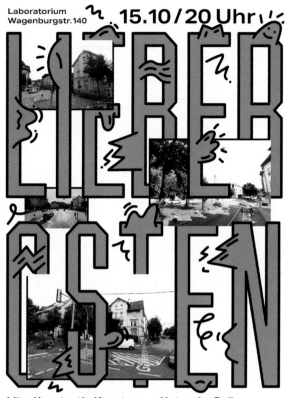

Laboratorium
Wagenburgstr. 140

15.10 / 20 Uhr

Mit **Konstantin Kenntner — Natascha Bell
Fuchs & Krüml — TiZiAN — Markus Grund**

Lieber Osten
2016 — Poster
Client: Laboratorium Stuttgart
Typeface: Customised,
Aktiv Grotesk (Dalton Maag)
Design: F
e
l
i
x
Bareis

This poster was designed for a new music festival in Stuttgart, featuring different music genres and new perspectives.

Laboratorium
Wagenburgstr. 140

03.11 / 20 Uhr

Mit **BANALI MOLOKO und FLORIAN BÜHLER
(RITUAL DIGITAL / WHITENOISE)
PANAJAH (SKA) und RASGARASGA (BALKAN)**

Laboratorium
Wagenburgstr. 140

03.12 / 20 Uhr

Mit **Bonosera (Blues/Desert) | Hawelka (Blues/
Psychedelic) Singapur Spezial (Indie-Punk-Rock)
Alyne (Parquet) Alexander Maier (Romantica)**

Hochschule Düsseldorf
University of Applied Sciences

Peter Behrens School of Arts
Fachbereich Architektur

HSD PBSA

Mit freundlicher
Unterstützung
der Landeshauptstadt
Düsseldorf

TALK SHOW

**Workshop
Intra/Extra Muros Woche**

29. Mai 2015 — 19:00 Uhr
Künstlerverein Malkasten,
Theatersaal
Jacobistraße 6a
40211 Düsseldorf

malkasten.org

Der Bausatz

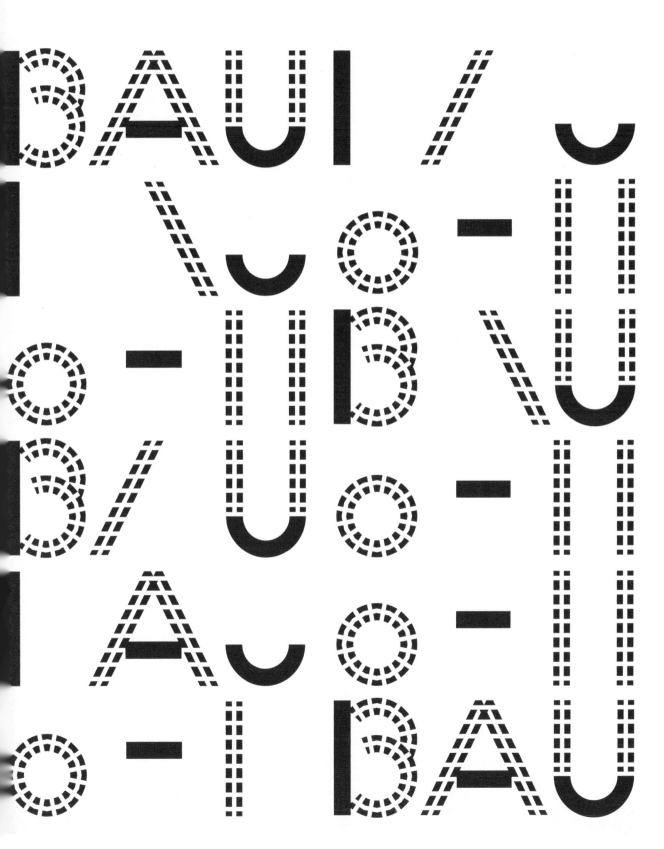

HSD Sans – Ein Universum an Möglichkeiten

Die HSD Sans ist ein Schriftentwurf, bei dem jeder Buchstabe aus dem gleichen Vorrat von vier verschiedenen Basiselementen entwickelt ist. Diese Basiselemente sind aus jeweils gleichartigen Modulen konstruiert. Hierdurch ergibt sich für alle Anwender des Corporate Designs die Möglichkeit, auf Basis dieses Formrepertoires „weiterzubauen". Grafiken, Illustrationen, Ornamente und vieles mehr gehören zu dem Universum an Möglichkeiten.

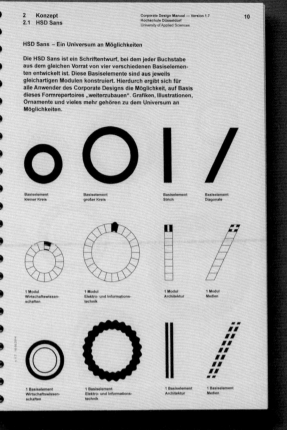

Basiselement kleiner Kreis

Basiselement großer Kreis

Basiselement Strich

Basiselement Diagonale

1 Modul Wirtschaftswissenschaften

1 Modul Elektro- und Informationstechnik

1 Modul Architektur

1 Modul Medien

1 Basiselement Wirtschaftswissenschaften

1 Basiselement Elektro- und Informationstechnik

1 Basiselement Architektur

1 Basiselement Medien

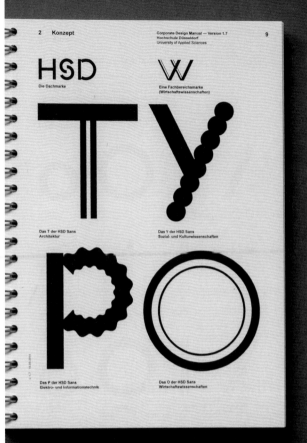

HSD
Die Dachmarke

W
Eine Fachbereichsmarke (Wirtschaftswissenschaften)

Das T der HSD Sans
Architektur

Das Y der HSD Sans
Sozial- und Kulturwissenschaften

Das P der HSD Sans
Elektro- und Informationstechnik

Das O der HSD Sans
Wirtschaftswissenschaften

HSD Sans Architektur

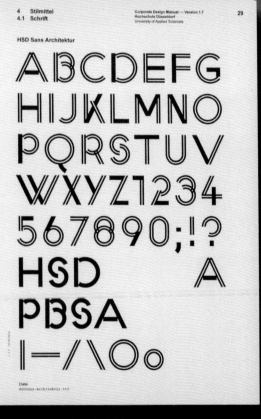

ABCDEFG
HIJKLMNO
PQRSTUV
WXYZ1234
567890;!?
HSD   A
PBSA
I—/\Oo

Datei
HSDSans-Architektur.ttf

HSD Sans Regular

ABCDEFG
HIJKLMNO
PQRSTUV
WXYZ1234
567890;!?
HSD

I—/\Oo

Datei
HSDSans-Regular.ttf

Hochschule Düsseldorf (HSD)
2015 — Visual Identity
Client: Hochschule Düsseldorf
Typeface: HSD Sans (Custom)

Design: Binger   Laucke   Siebein

For Hochschule Düsseldorf (University of Applied Sciences), the studio developed a new corporate design system that could easily be managed through typography. HSD Sans was created as a modular display typeface inspired by the basic elements of Milton Glaser's Stencil type, which has been used in the university's corporate design. Its strong appearance represents the university itself, whereas the seven styles reflect the different faculties.

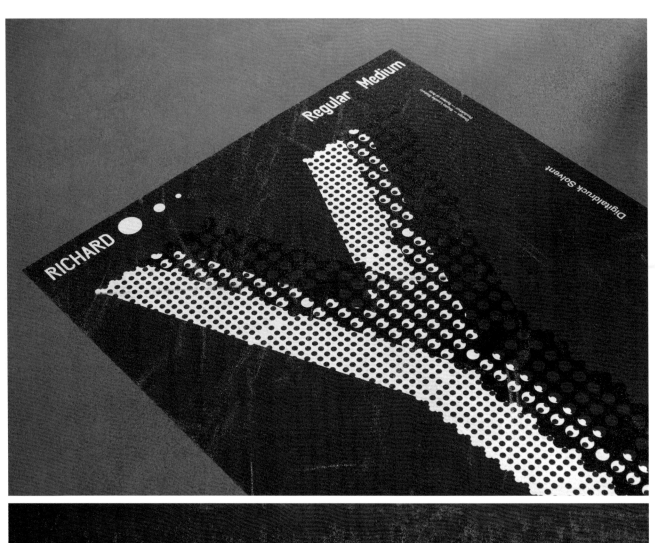

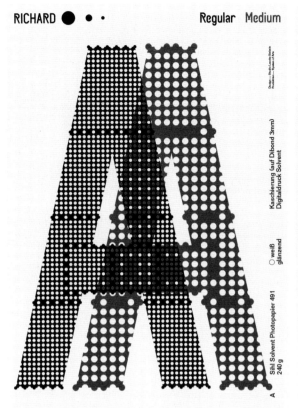

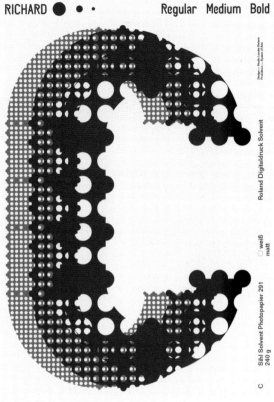

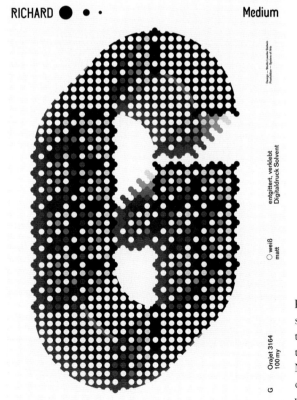

Richard; From A to Z
2016 — Visual Identity
Typeface: Richard (Custom)
Design: Binger Laucke Siebein

Richard is a modular display typeface consisting of three styles: Regular, Medium, Bold. The dimensions of the letters do not grow by weight, but by the size of the perforation in their own grid system. For the Nachtschicht Design Night exhibition, this series of 26 specimen posters was produced to show the potential of the typeface in combination with multiple digital production techniques.

2016, 17 — Poster
Client: Yale University School of Art
and Studienstiftung des Deutschen Volkes
Typeface: Visuelt (The Entente, Colophon)

Design: Franci   Virgili

Stephen Chen

"Managing Financial Affairs After Master of Fine Art"

Friday, 4/28
3.30pm
Room 204
Yale School of Art
36 Edgewood Ave.

During this discussion, Stephen will discuss topics of budgeting finances, credit stability, differences of tax forms such as W2, W9 and 1099, student loan repayment, income tax and health insurance. With a "Q&A" following the lecture. Open to undergraduates and graduate students of all years.

Designed for specific events at YALE University in 2016-2017, these posters were a manifestation of the designer's personal exploration in coming to terms with his own style – visually and methodologically. Around recurring visual elements, the typography takes up all the space that is left; sporadically and playfully interacting with them or ignoring them overall.

2017 — Poster
Client: Zefir 7 / Koos Breen
Typeface: Custom,
Tacite (Pauline Le Pape)

Design: Sepus   Noordmans

This poster was designed for the Zefir 7 event at Stroom Den Haag, featuring one talk by Michiel Schuurman. In bringing this poster to life, the designer created his own personal method of working based on the works of Schuurman himself. By not being restricted by the format of the canvas, he was able to manifest the result of his experiments.

States of Play:

R
o
l
e
p
l
a

y

Reality
2018—Identity

Client: FACT (Foundation for Art and Creative Technology), Liverpool, UK
Typeface: Clip (Asger Behncke Jacobsen and Mads Wildgaard, Bold Decisions),
Lars (Mads Wildgaard, Bold Decisions)
Design: The Rodina

The States of Play exhibition visual identity was extended from a video game offering an alternative vision of reality, reflecting the fact that games are often perceived as a means of escape for the player – an immersion into another world. Although it is increasingly harder to separate the make-believe from reality, the interplay between the real and virtual is inescapable. Using the landscapes, mechanics, and cultures in gaming to reveal how the power dynamics of the physical world also exist in make-believe, the exhibition explored games as both liberating and limiting spaces in which to reflect and re-imagine the world, and how differing visions of the world can oppose one another. Design: The Rodina; Artwork: Reija Merilainen.

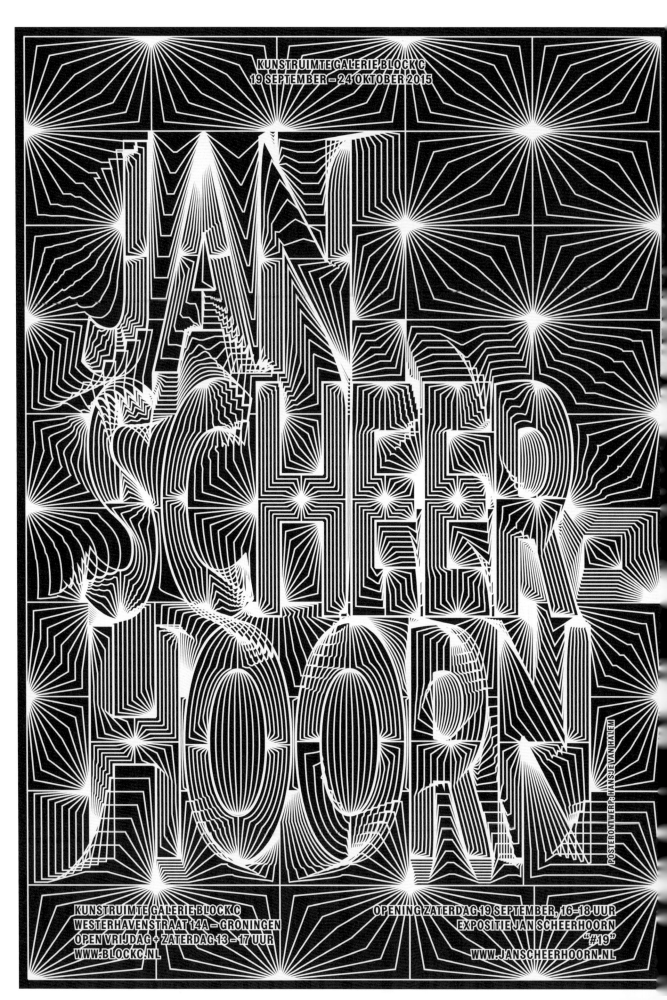

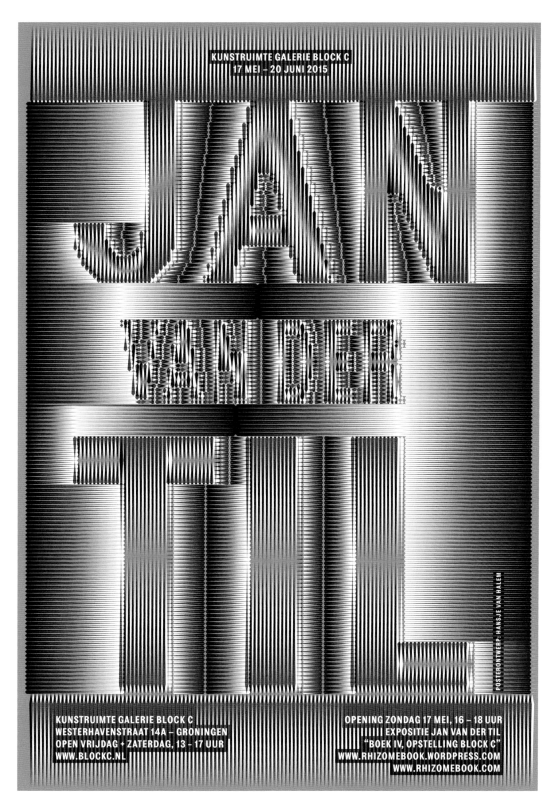

Galerie BlockC (Jan Scheerhoorn and Jan van der Til)
2015 — Posters
Client: Galerie Block C, Groningen
Typeface: Custom
Design: Hansje van Halem Studio

These posters were designed for an artist-run gallery, and served as a means of research for the studio.

Lowlands Festival
2017, 18 — Visual Identity

Client: Lowlands Festival, MOJO
Typeface: Custom

Design: Hansje van
Halem Studio

The custom design software for Lowlands transforms shapes and letters
into a horizontal and vertical line pattern. Parameters can be modified and
even animated to generate different
artwork like posters, advertising,
signage, merchandise, animations as
well as an additional static font.

2017 — Typeface
Client: Typotheque.com
Typeface: Wind (Hansje van Halem, Typotheque)
Design: Hansje van Halem Studio

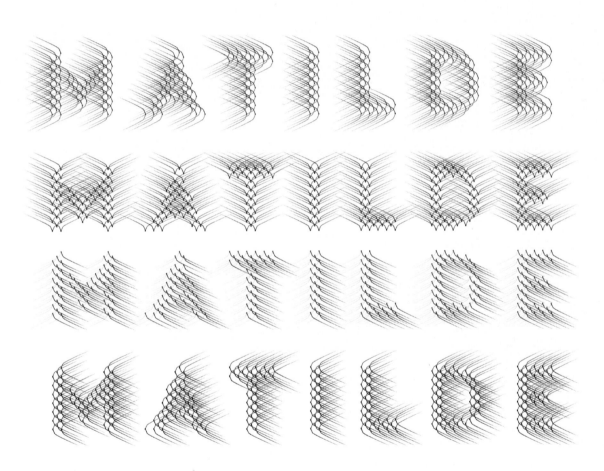

Various layers can be combined and layered to create vibrant, hypnotic patterns. As such, Wind is both a typeface and a tool for graphic expression; intuitive and systematic in exploring the limits of legibility and the differences between reading and viewing.

Besides the four static styles (NE, SE, SW and NE), Wind also includes variable fonts capable of rotating a full 360° (clockwise and anti-clockwise), offering unprecedented possibilities for the experimentation of repetitive textural patterns.

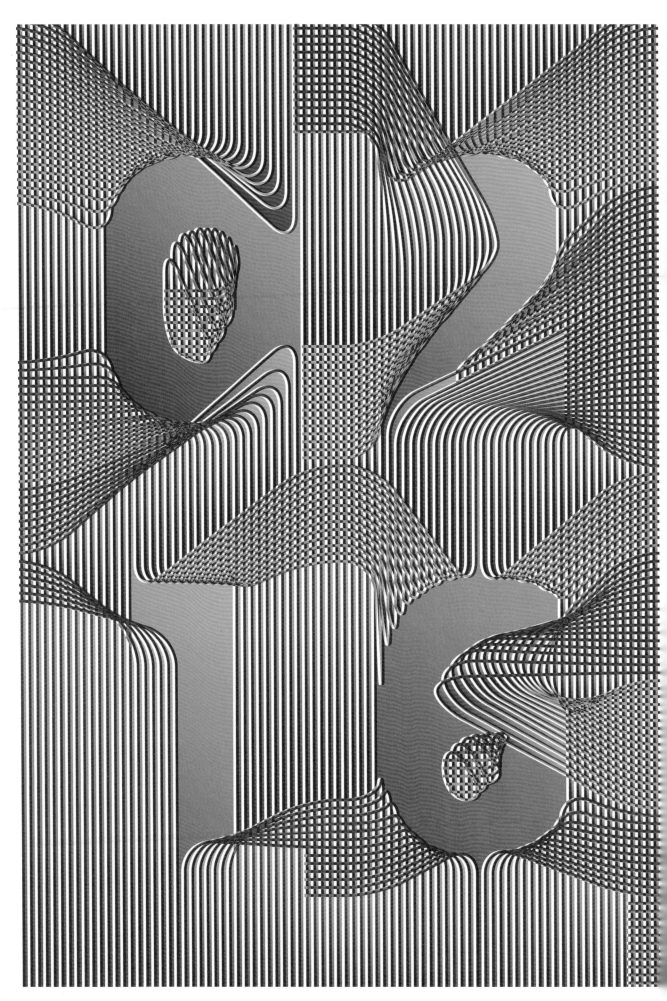

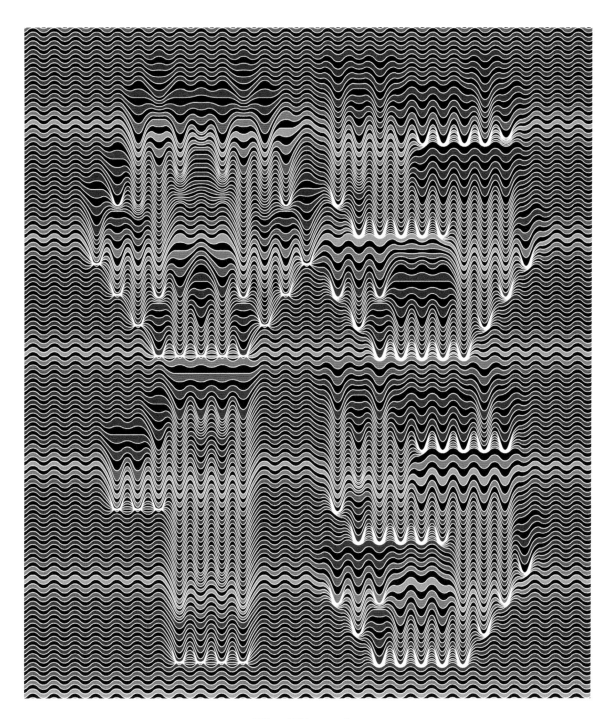

Wired Illustration

Client: Wired Germany
Typeface: Custom
Design: Hansje van Halem Studio

This illustration was created for a column in Wired magazine.

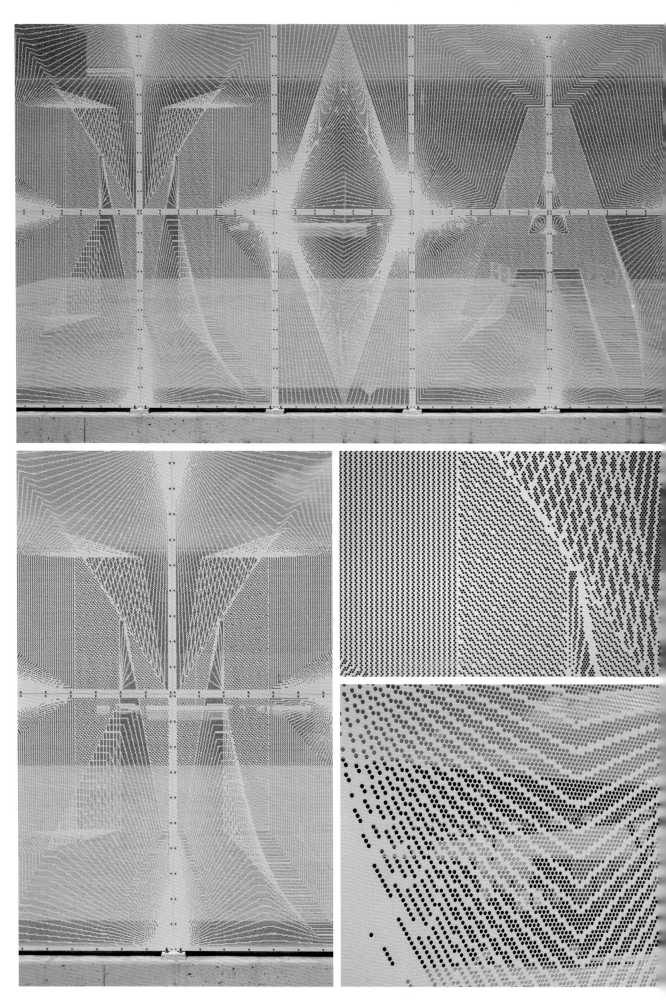

SmartGate
2016 — Environmental Graphics
Client: SmartGate, Schiphol Airport
Typeface: Custom
Design: Hansje van Halem Studio

This artwork was commissioned for the new SmartGate building at Schipol Airport where cargo is scanned. When the pattern on the fence is "scanned", the word "SmartGate" appears.

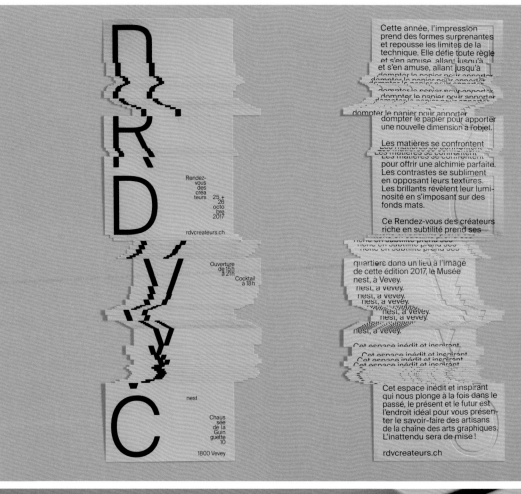

N
R
D
Y
C

Rendez-
vous
des
créa-
teurs

25 +
26
octo
bre
2017

rdvcreateurs.ch

Ouverture
de 15h
à 21h

Cocktail
à 18h

nest

Chaus
sée
de la
Guin
guette
10

1800 Vevey

Cette année, l'impression prend des formes surprenantes et repousse les limites de la technique. Elle défie toute règle et s'en amuse, allant jusqu'à dompter le papier pour apporter une nouvelle dimension à l'objet.

Les matières se confrontent pour offrir une alchimie parfaite. Les contrastes se subliment en opposant leurs textures. Les brillants révèlent leur luminosité en s'imposant sur des fonds mats.

Ce Rendez-vous des créateurs riche en subtilité prend ses quartiers dans un lieu à l'image de cette édition 2017, le Musée nest, à Vevey.

Cet espace inédit et inspirant qui nous plonge à la fois dans le passé, le présent et le futur est l'endroit idéal pour vous présenter le savoir-faire des artisans de la chaîne des arts graphiques. L'inattendu sera de mise !

rdvcreateurs.ch

Graphic design atelier Balmer Hählen has been tasked by nine craftsmen in the graphic arts industry to design the communication materials for the "Rendez-vous des créateurs" events. In 2017, Balmer Hählen began designing the invitations by asking themselves: "What if impression took over graphics?" At that point, it was possible to come up with surprising forms and push the limits of techniques in printing. All rules could be defied, and new dimensions could be added onto an object by tampering with the paper used. As a result, the atelier could showcase its expertise in printing through their limited-edition invitation card design, with only 3,000 total copies printed. Its clever use of various papers demonstrated the card's high quality, with cut-outs, textures, a glossy varnish, and hot-printed matter taking over and modifying the typography.

Each material confronted another to offer a perfect alchemy, making contrasts sublime through the play of textures and shiny effects more luminous on matte surfaces.

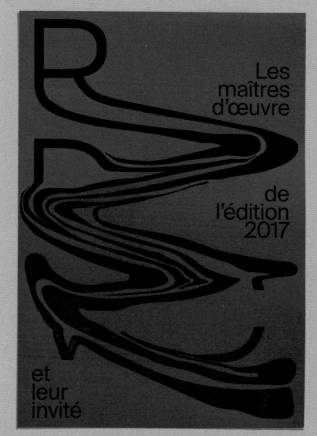

Les
maîtres
d'œuvre

de
l'édition
2017

et
leur
invité

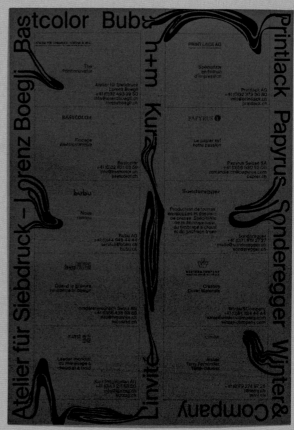

The YellowPress Periodical developed out of a growing need to make the multifaceted research culture of the St. Lucas School of Arts Antwerp accessible to a wider audience. Its editorial board gathers content once a year, and selects the most interesting contributions to be published in the magazine. For every output, a launch is staged and involves an evening of talks and performances. The release of issue 4 was approached as if it were a movie festival, with the magazine content repurposed to resemble the tagline for an upcoming movie premiere and placed onto a moving flag. The act of promoting a magazine without actually showing how it looks created a sense of vagueness that was more than appealing.

**Campus
Ultzama**
02.07—
12.07.2018

02.07—12.07.2018
Workshop 1
Francisco Mangado

02.07—12.07.2018
Workshop 2
Eduardo Souto
de Moura

Presentation

The Fundación Arquitectura y Sociedad is a non-profit, private cultural entity with a national and international reach. Based in Madrid and Pamplona, it was set up in 2008 with the aim of promoting architecture as a field inextricably bound to life in society at large. An annual activity of the organization is Campus Ultzama, held in the Navarrese municipality of Ultzama.

School

Directors: **Carlos Pereda, Ignacio Olite**

The Summer School consists of two Workshops to be held simultaneously, side by side, immediately after the Encounters. Students will work with three professors in developing a single project based on the program set. The idea is to give the students the opportunity to work in a set-up resembling that of a real-life practice tasked with a commission, under the supervision of the professors. Emphasis will be on "with," rather than on "for," simulating the intensity and efficiency of team work in an architectural office as well as the journey through the various phases of a project, from design to execution.

Workshop 1
02.07—12.07.2018
Professors: **Francisco Mangado, Carlos Pereda, Ignacio Olite**

Workshop 2
02.07—12.07.2018
Professors: **Eduardo Souto de Moura, Camilo Rebelo, João Pedro Serodio**

Maximum number of students per Workshop: 9
Total number of students: 18

Students: The workshop is thought out for students in their fifth year of their architecture degree program or in the process of completing their thesis projects, but also recent graduates (with less than two years of work experience).

Theme: Humanize the City: The Elderly. Spaces for Living and Working.

Applications: Send to **info@arquitecturaysociedad.com** a short graphic portfolio (max. 2 A3-size pages) and a letter (1 A4-size page) stating your reasons for seeking admission. The selection of students will be done before June 17rd.

Deadline for submitting applications: June 8th, 2018

Location and accommodations: Ultzama Equestrian Center. Students will work and stay at this facility, surrounded by nature.

Languages: English and Spanish.

Excursions: Students can expect to visit the construction site at least once. Likewise, at least two excursions are organized to get to know the contemporary architecture of the Basque Country and Navarra. Kursaal (San Sebastián), Archeology Museum (Vitoria), Chillida Leku Museum (Hernani, Guipúzcoa), Oteiza Foundation-Museum (Alzuza-Navarra).

Sanfermines: On July 13 and 14, students, if they consider it convenient, can enjoy the San Fermín festival in Pamplona.

Tuition: The amount payable of 3,000 € includes tuition and bed & board, plus the excursion to the construction site.

Information and applications:
www.arquitecturaysociedad.org
info@arquitecturaysociedad.com

This poster was designed for Campus Ultzama, an institution in Spain focusing on promoting architecture. The typographic work aimed to communicate the nature of the materials as well as the architectural values of the building where the courses being promoted in the poster take place.

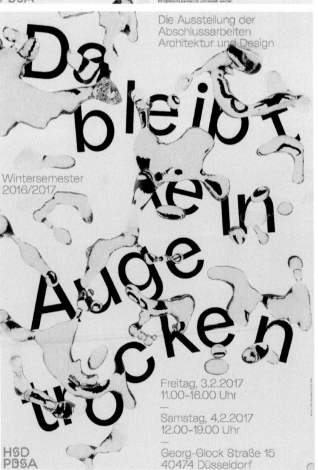

Graduation

Event 2017

2017 — Visual Identity
Client: Hochschule Düsseldorf /
University of Applied Sciences Düsseldorf
Typeface: La Nord (Raoul Gottschling,
Type Club Düsseldorf)
Design: Raoul Gottschling
and Tobias Hönow

Joy, frustration, and fear — emotions that make graduates break into sweat while working on their final projects, only to bring tears of happiness into their eyes when they finally hold their diplomas in their hands. For Hochschule Düsseldorf's visual identity in 2017, these biological fluids were visually translated into key elements across communication materials, interacting with a layer of Raoul Gottschling's La Nord typeface, which was developed simultaneously.

EUROPE

Brando Corradini x Monday Poster
05.05.2017

This poster was created for Poster Monday, a weekly feature on the Poster Poster website featuring the best work submitted by designers around the world. The concept behind this design represents the will and need to unite the peoples of Europe, as represented completely and graphically by the word "Europe", which gradually distorts and almost disintegrates towards the lower part of the poster. The underlying message is that the peoples should remain unique under the same flag without economic ties and racial or religious discrimination.

Through A Glass Darkly
UIC School of Design
2017–18 Public Seminar Series
TILL WITTWER
Thursday, November 9, 6:00PM
Free and Open to the Public

Room 1100
UIC School of Design
College of Architecture,
Design, and the Arts
845 West Harrison Street
Chicago

This series of seminars aims to investigate the parameters of design as a practice. Rather than showcasing "best practices"—optimal ways for designers to take on predetermined roles—it looks at alternative models for the profession in which designers develop their own agendas and territories.

As a field, design has changed dramatically over the past few decades. While Modernist designers worked to rationalize their output in the 1950s and 60s, Postmodernism shattered that seemingly objective (yet authoritative) Modernist world view in the 1980s and 90s. Postmodernism's lack of agenda, alongside the democratization of production tools and the World Wide Web, allowed for the nostalgic return of Modernism as a so-called "Global Style"/"Zombie Modernism" in the early 2000's, but without early Modernism's sense of public mission and service. Now the question is: where do we stand as design practitioners, writers, and educators in the post-digital and post-internet era? How do we redefine the role of the contemporary designer?

Through a Glass Darkly questions notions of design practice today by considering alternative agendas for design. It showcases practices that go beyond surface, image, and form and utilize design as a tool capable of generating references and agendas outside predetermined boundaries. It introduces designers that elevate design discourse by repurposing design in the form of writing, producing, and publishing. It brings together designers who reject the status quo and seek to create their own alternative realities; designers who endeavor to remain relevant by redefining their practice and adopting positions outside traditionally defined domains.

In his 1961 feature film Through a Glass Darkly, Ingmar Bergman portrays a character named Karin who has returned to her estranged family after being institutionalized for a period of time. Karin's husband, brother, and father live on a tiny island. While living with them, Karin begins to hear voices and eventually can no longer differentiate between reality and her imagined world. It becomes clear to Karin that she cannot live successfully in both realities. Eventually, she agrees to be institutionalized again in order to continue living her own fiction.

This series of seminars aims to investigate the parameters of design as a practice. Rather than showcasing "best practices"—optimal ways for designers to take on predetermined roles—it looks at alternative models for the profession in which designers develop their own agendas and territories./// As a field, design has changed dramatically over the past few decades. While Modernist designers worked to rationalize their output in the 1950s and 60s, Postmodernism shattered that seemingly objective (yet authoritative) Modernist world view in the 1980s and 90s. Postmodernism's lack of agenda, alongside the democratization of production tools and the World Wide Web, allowed for the nostalgic return of Modernism as a so-called "Global Style"/"Zombie Modernism" in the early 2000's, but without early Modernism's sense of public mission and service. Now the question is: where do we stand as design practitioners, writers, and educators in the post-digital and post-internet era? How do we redefine the role of the contemporary designer?///Through a Glass Darkly questions notions of design practice today by considering alternative agendas for design. It showcases practices that go beyond surface, image, and form and utilize design as a tool capable of generating references and agendas outside predetermined boundaries. It introduces designers that elevate design discourse by repurposing design in the form of writing, producing, and publishing. It brings together designers who reject the status quo and seek to create their own alternative realities; designers who endeavor to remain relevant by redefining their practice and adopting positions outside traditionally defined domains.

Through A Glass Darkly
UIC School of Design 2017–18
Public Seminar Series
ANDREW BLAUVELT
Thursday, February 1, 6:00PM
Free and Open to the Public

Room 1100
UIC School of Design
College of Architecture,
Design, and the Arts
845 West Harrison Street
Chicago

In his 1961 feature film Through a Glass Darkly, Ingmar Bergman portrays a character named Karin who has returned to her estranged family after being institutionalized for a period of time. Karin's husband, brother, and father live on a tiny island. While living with them, Karin begins to hear voices and eventually can no longer differentiate between reality and her imagined world. It becomes clear to Karin that she cannot live successfully in both realities. Eventually, she agrees to be institutionalized again in order to continue living her own fiction.

Through A Glass Darkly
2017, 18 — Visual Identity
Client: University of Illinois at Chicago, School of Design

Typeface:

Arges (Matthieu Salvaggio, Blaze Type), Shakotan (Benoît Brun),
Kraft (Jacob Wise), Suisse I'ntl (Swiss Typefaces), Nemesis,
Asfalt, Knife Mono (A is for Apple), Pano (Filip Matějíček, Heavyweigh),
Engravers Old English (Morris Fuller Benton), LL Brown (Aurèle Sack, Lineto)
Design: Pouya Ahmadi

These posters were designed for Through A Glass Darkly, a series of four public seminars at the UIC School of Design in 2017/2018 that aimed to investigate the parameters of design as a practice. Rather than showcasing the "best practices" or optimal ways for designers to take on predetermined roles, it looked at alternative models for the profession in which designers could develop their own agendas and territories. It also showcased practices that go beyond surface, image, and form by utilising design as a tool capable of generating references and agendas outside predetermined boundaries. Each featured designer elevated the design discourse by repurposing design in the form of writing, producing, and publishing.

Nike Apparel
2018 — Typographic Identity
Client: Nike
Typeface: Futura (Paul Renner)
Design: Dia

These generative typographic elements and patterns were designed for the Nike 2019 sportswear identity.

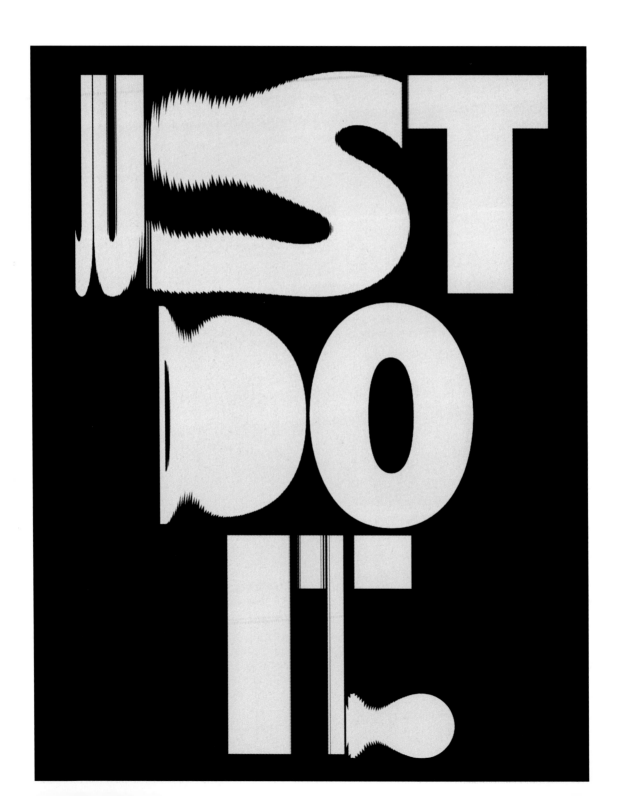

Album Art for Manifeste contre la peur
2017 — Album
Client: Viole TT Pi
Typeface: Druk (Berton Hasebe, Commercial Type),
Ogg (Lucas Sharp and Greg Gazdowicz)
Design: Julien Hébert and David Beauchemin

Violett Pi is the project of Karl Gagnon, a musician who stands out in Quebec with an eclectic style that spans everything from nü metal to psychedelic poetry. His album "Manifeste contre la peur" (Manifesto Against Fear) deals with themes such as self-censorship and the fear of proclaiming himself as an artist. In this self-portrait, he confronts his truth through various typographic treatments inspired by his contemporary yet baroque style.

NYC NYC Streets
Wants LOOKING CIT
IT WATC
All NYC OU
Wants Wants
IT HEADO
All All
WE WE Want Our NAME ON The BACK
CITY On THE Front RING
FINGER CHAMPAGNE On OUR Shirt

Nike Statement House NYC
2018 — Visual Identity
Client: Nike
Typeface: Druk (Berton Hasebe, Commercial Type),
Rhymes (Stanley Morison and Jakub Samek)

D   e   s   i   g   n   :   Dia

These experiential typographic animations were
created for Nike's Statement House event.

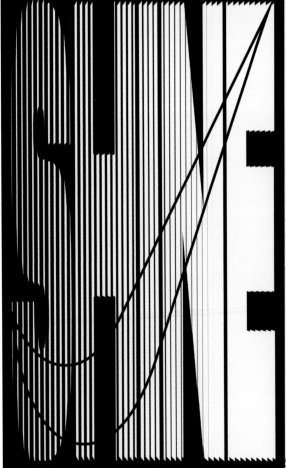

RISE
GRIND
AGAIN
AGAIN
AGAIN
AGAIN AGAIN
AGAIN AGAIN
AGAIN AGAIN
AGAIN AGAIN
AGAIN AGAIN

KDII Shoe
2018 — Typographic Identity
Client: Nike
Typeface: Druk (Berton Hasebe, Commercial Type)

Design:

This typographic identity was designed for Kevin Durant's KDII shoe.

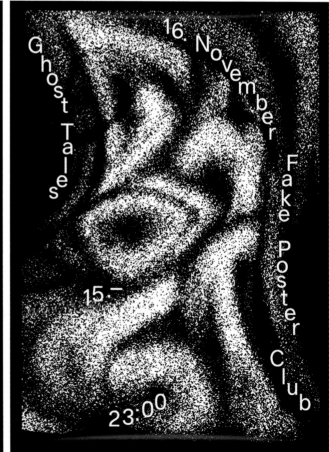

MORE MORE MORE
Fake Poster Club
5. Juli 2016
23.00 h
15.–

Fake Poster Club
2016 till now — Poster
Typeface: Funktional Grotesk (Davide Rossetto)
Design: Kevin Hoegger

Every time Kevin Hoegger discovers a new technique for creating words or letters, he visualises and designs a fictional gig poster. Although Kevin always includes the same gig details, he only changes the name of the band, which forms the basis for typography. Over the years, Kevin Hoegger has amassed a small collection of work; a few of which have been shown publicly at various venues.

ICI
L'ONDE

2016 SEPT
—
DÉC

DIJON

WHY
NOTE

Conception graphique : Atelier Tout va bien
Sérigraphie : Lézard graphique

Musique
au centre d'art
Le Consortium

I   C   I   L   '   OOO   NNN   DDD   EEE

2016, 17 — Visual Identity
Client: Association Why Note
Typeface: Custom, Sans Text (Klim Type)
Design: Atelier Tout va bien

This visual identity for the experimental music department at Le Consortium, the Dijon-based art centre, was designed using only paper: the rawest, most affordable creative material. To reflect the fact that sound forms the basis – or main "material" – of this department's functions, the designers had to crease, cut, rip, and fold sheets of paper, resulting in the creation of brutalist letters. Subsequently, they also designed a poster series for the Why Note for Ici l'Onde programme.

6'56"
www.6m56s.com

6'56" was originally founded by Jurgen Maelfeyt who has been running his own studio since 2005. In 2010, he started Art Paper Editions and then opened riot in 2014. 6'56" does art direction, editorial design, graphic design, web design and development, as well as workshops and lectures. It works with institutions and brands such as Belgian Pavillion Venice Biennale Architecture, 51n4e, Art Paper Editions, Be-Part, Ghent Art Book Fair, Kask, Maarten Van Severen Foundation, riot, Sofie d'Hoore, Sternberg Press, Toneelhuis, vai, as well as artists such as Hilde Bouchez, Ruth Van Beek, Tom Callemin, Bieke Depoorter, Pieterjan Ginckels, Jan Hoek, Paul Kooiker, Renzo Martens, Hana Miletic, Max Pinckers and Mariken Wessels, amongst others.
— pp. 152-153

A Black Cover Design
www.ablackcover.com

A Black Cover Design (abbr. ABCD) is a small creative studio specialising in graphic design. It is based in Beijing, China, and was founded in 2015. ABCD delivers branding, visual identity, product packaging, user interface, and printed matter design, as well as design-driven strategy services to clients and their audiences. Their work demonstrates a design philosophy that reflects exceptional, systematic, and pertinent communication methodology, while winning their clients' recognition and numerous international and domestic awards.
— pp. 150-151

Any Studio
www.any.studio

Any Studio is a new kind of creative agency combining the aesthetic momentum and flexibility of a young design office with strategic expertise and a human-centric service approach. As designers, they do not limit themselves to anything in particular – based on creative approaches, bold visual concepts, and usability, they strive towards challenges that matter. As consultants, the team shares their expertise in design thinking and brand strategy, seeking to gain experiences together with their clients and benefit from mutual involvement.
— pp. 176-177

A Practice for Everyday Life
apracticeforeverydaylife.com

A Practice for Everyday Life is a graphic design studio based in London. Their work includes art direction, identities, publications, exhibitions, type design, signage, packaging, and digital design. They have built a reputation as an internationally renowned and sought-after collaborator through working with like-minded companies, galleries, institutions, and individuals. Their design philosophy stems from a conceptual rigour that ensures each design is meaningful and original.
— pp. 72-73

Artem Matyushkin
www.a-r-t-e-m.com

Artem Matyushkin is an art director and multidisciplinary designer born in Moscow and based in New York. His practice is mostly focused on creating visual identities and designing editorial experiences. Throughout his work, the core elements always remain the same – namely typography, colours, and shapes.
— pp. 202-203

Atelier Tout va bien
www.ateliertoutvabien.com

Atelier Tout va bien are Anna Chevance and Mathias Reynoird, who started collaborating in 2011 in Dijon. The atelier works mainly in cultural fields on visual identities, posters, and books while embracing all printed matter.
— pp. 88-89, 126-127, 258-259

Aurelia Peter
www.aureliapeter.ch

Aurelia Peter is a Swiss graphic designer based in St.Gallen and Zurich. She works on various projects, most of them in the cultural field, with typography being a central aspect of her work. Aurelia grew up in St.Gallen, Switzerland, where she later completed her apprenticeship as a graphic designer. Because of ger passion and fascination for graphic design, she sought to deepen and expand her knowledge by studying visual communication at the Zurich University of the Arts (ZHDK). Aurelia is graduating in summer 2019 from ZHDK.
— pp. 104-105, 166-167

Balmer Hählen
www.balmerhahlen.ch

Founded in 2011 by Priscilla Balmer and Yvo Hählen and established since 2013 in the heart of Lausanne, the studio started under the name, A3 Studio, to become Balmer Hählen in 2017. Since its founding, the studio has been involved in various collaborations, especially with designers, stylists, artists, and photographers. Its ongoing artistic explorations allow the team to develop different types of print, digital, and three-dimensional media; resulting in work that is regularly awarded in Switzerland and abroad. Its posters have been selected and exhibited several times at international competitions in countries such as Japan, China, Russia, Scotland, and for four consecutive years, at "100 Beste Plakate" or the 100 Best Posters competition in Germany, Austria, and Switzerland. Besides graphic design, Balmer Hählen also helms its own artistic production projects.
— pp. 238-241

Beetroot Design Group
www.beetroot.gr

Beetroot Design Group is a Thessaloniki-based, multi-awarded communication design office and think tank that provides design services and solutions to a worldwide clientele. The team consists of experts with a wide and diverse range of skills in the creative field; all operating under the creative mission to discover, develop, and utilise the true essence of a brand, product, or service – ultimately growing and expanding it into being recognised, appreciated, and praised all around the globe.
— pp. 98-101

Bernd Volmer
www.berndvolmer.com

Bernd works as Font Engineer, Type Designer, and Project Manager at Monotype in Berlin. He goes back and forth between tech and design, exploring and reviving old technology with his Pen Plotter Lab.
— pp. 122-123

Bilal Sebei
bilalsebei.com

Bilal is a graphic designer and art director based in Lausanne, Switzerland, where he graduated with honours in the Master Art Direction (Type Option) programme at ECAL. He specialises in graphic design for print, web, branding, and motion graphics with a strong focus on typography. Currently, he works in the cultural and commercial fields for companies and individuals, as well as on self-initiated projects.
— pp. 48-49, 132-133

Binger Laucke Siebein
www.binger-laucke-siebein.com

Binger Laucke Siebein stands for progressive and nonconformist concepts, communication, and design. The agency works internationally from Berlin and Amsterdam, under the direction of Daniel Binger, Dirk Laucke, and Johanna Siebein who specialise in creative strategies, brand development and dynamic identities for cultural as well as commercial clients. They combine a strategic approach with high-quality design across different print and digital platforms.
— pp. 188-189, 218-223

Brando Corradini
www.brandocorradinigrafik.info

Brando Corradini is a graphic designer who is passionate about his work. He draws inspiration from everything that surrounds him and from every experience. Brando lives by the philosophy that "anything that surrounds us is visual communication". He believes that good graphics should communicate with just a little, not by adding but by selecting. His design motto is "less is more", which as a mantra, guides him through a job.
— pp. 50-51, 114, 138, 158-159, 246

Braulio Amado Design Studio
www.badbadbadbad.com

Braulio Amado is a Portuguese graphic designer living in New York who started his own design studio in 2017. His clients include Frank Ocean, Washed Out, Roisin Murpy, Apple, Nike, Wired, and The New York Times.
— pp. 196-200

Build
www.studio.build

Build is an award-winning creative studio with an international reputation for creating strong visual narratives. Utilising art direction and graphic design, they create brand identities, websites, packaging, and books for design-led clients around the world.
— p. 130

Building Paris
www.buildingparis.fr

Building Paris is an office for communication and design run by Benoît Santiard and Guillaume Grall based in Paris.
— p. 112-113

Bureau Bordeaux
www.bureaubordeaux.com

Bureau Bordeaux is a studio for content and design. It develops, edits, and designs magazines, books, corporate publications, websites and identities. With a focus on art direction and concepts, it creates projects that occupy the space between art, design, and advertising.
— pp. 42-43

museums, such as the Stedelijk Museum Amsterdam.
— pp. 228-237

Helmo
www.helmo.fr

Thomas and Clément met in 1997 during their studies in Besançon. Both went their own ways in 1999, in Paris, but founded La Bonne Merveille, a graphic design studio, in 2003 with T. Dimetto. After splitting up in 2007, Thomas and Clément continued their collaboration as a duo under the name Helmo. Currently, they work in various fields of graphic design, mainly for cultural institutions or festivals in France. The studio's body of work plays with concepts like variation, mutation, randomness, and combination. Helmo is based in Montreuil, France.
— pp. 90-91

Ines Cox
www.inescox.com

Ines Cox runs her own independent graphic design studio in Antwerp. In 2009, she graduated from Luca School of Arts in Ghent, with a degree in graphic design and continued studying for a second master's course at Werkplaats Typografie in The Netherlands. Specialising in printed matter and graphic identities, she has completed a wide variety of projects for clients ranging from independent artists and galleries to brands, schools, and museums. Ines also teaches typography at the graphic design department of the Royal Academy in Antwerp, and has been a researcher there since January 2017.
— pp. 40-41, 68-69, 156-157

Ivo Brouwer
www.ivobrouwer.com
www.highontype.com

Ivo Brouwer is a (typo-)graphic designer and a teacher of letter making. His work varies from animated letters, bespoke typefaces, and posters to identities. He always starts his assignments from scratch, with brand-new made type. Inspired by street signage, psychedelic images, and comics, his visuals are often on the verge of aesthetically pleasing and hurtful to the eyes. Besides working for clients, Ivo creates uncommissioned work to learn and perfect new tricks. Due to his curiosity in the ever-changing typographic landscape, he spends time teaching graphic design at universities in the Netherlands. Together with High on Type, he organises events, initiates projects, and travels the world sharing knowledge about type and calligraphy.
— pp. 128-129

Jim Kühnel
www.jimkuehnel.net

Jim Kühnel is a studio for graphic design in Leipzig, Germany, that specialises in editorial design, visual identities, and art direction. It primarily works with artists, institutions, galleries, labels, and publishers.
— p. 165

Julien Hébert
and David Beauchemin
www.julienhebert.net

Based in Montréal, Julien and David are involved in typography and image making. Their work crosses many disciplines, from branding to website design as well as editorial design; approaching every project with the passion and desire to make something great.
— pp. 102-103, 251

Kevin Hoegger
www.kevinhoegger.allyou.net

Kevin is a Swiss designer based in Zürich but working in almost every corner of the world. His interests lie not only in typography and systematic graphic design, but also in branding that goes much further than just printed matter. Additionally, he works on signage, interiors, and furniture projects.
— pp. 56-57, 256-257

Koln Studio
kolnstudio.com

Founded in 2014, Koln Studio fronts every type of project, seeking unique solutions for every customer and working hand in hand. It works for institutions, businesses, and private customers on projects across different scales. Its aim is to offer global and lasting outcomes, working from the initial idea up to the final production – looking for original and solid concepts that provide a design strategy and enrichment.
— pp. 28-29, 124

Lamm & Kirch
www.lamm-kirch.com

Lamm & Kirch are a graphic design studio focusing on the creation of books, visual identities, and exhibitions in the broad cultural sector. It mostly does printed matter with an approach defined by continuous co-operation in shifting constellations. The studio likes the old and the new, the obvious and the hidden; functioning as a research facility to explore visual language. Its idea of working is defined by working "with" instead of "for" somebody. Lamm & Kirch's work has been awarded

at the International Poster Festival, Chaumont, and with the most beautiful Swiss books. Besides winning at the "100 Beste Plakate" several times, it was also recognised with "Schönste deutsche Bücher" in 2008 and the Walter-Tiemann-Price in 2010. In 2014 and 2018, the studio was also shortlisted for the Walter-Tiemann-Price.
— pp. 52-53, 181

Mainstudio
(Edwin Van Gelder)
www.mainstudio.com

Mainstudio is an Amsterdam-based graphic design studio founded by Edwin van Gelder in 2005. The studio creates projects derived from the intersection of art and architecture across mediums including publications, digital media, and visual identities. Each piece of work is characterised by a content-driven editorial approach, and led by systematic design. Mainstudio has been honoured with extensive international awards, including the "Best Book Design from all over the World" (2013), the "Best Dutch Book Design" (2011, 2012, 2016, and 2017) and the "Art Directors Club New York" (2009).
— pp. 44-47, 64-65, 160-161

Mateo Broillet
www.mateobroillet.ch

Mateo Broillet is a graphic designer with a strong focus on typography and editorial projects. After graduating in visual communication from ECAL in 2014, Mateo worked in Berlin, Geneva, and Amsterdam where he settled to study in the design department at the Sandberg Instituut.
— p. 164, 194-195

Milkxhake
www.milkxhake.org

Milkxhake is an independent graphic design studio located in Hong Kong. Founded in 2006 by Javin Mo, Milkxhake advocates the power of visual communication from visual branding, identity, print, and website design. By bringing up creative ideas and unique visual languages, the studio focuses on the creative process while delivering messages to its collaborators as well as the public community. Starting from a very small-scale practice, Milkxhake has stirred the community's imagination over the years, and has attracted a growing number of leading local and international clients. The studio has won numerous international design awards.
— pp. 134-135

Murmure
www.murmure.me

Based in Caen and Paris, Murmure is a French creative communications agency specialising in strong visual identities. Led by art directors Julien Alirol Ressencourt and Paul, the agency produces singular creative projects with aesthetics adapted to its customers' problems. It responds to the client's aims and objectives; guiding and advising them in order to provide them with original, creative, and aesthetic projects that it can be proud of.
— pp. 34-35, 116-117

Naranjo–Etxeberria
www.naranjoetxeberria.com

Naranjo–Etxeberria is constantly changing. It is not a design studio, but a group of creative minds that work on contemporary visual culture with a strong base on concepts. Established in 2014 and based in Madrid, N–E is a flexible team that collaborate with professional talent selected by mutual empathy and admiration which results in a multidisciplinary approach adjustable to all kinds of projects from different fields. Each part of N–E plays a different role, but everyone pursues a single, common goal: to solve every project in the best and unique possible way.
— pp. 84-85, 118-119

Nolan Paparelli
www.nolan-paparelli.ch

Nolan Paparelli is a Swiss graphic designer offering services in editorial design, visual identity, and type design. He graduated with honours from ECAL/University of Art and Design of Lausanne in 2015 and has since worked on various projects, mainly in the cultural field, including collaborations with Editions Attinger, Le Grand 8, Herburg Weiland, Kairos Studio, and Swiss Typefaces.
— pp. 120-121, 125

Offshore Studio
www.offshorestudio.ch

Offshore Studio is a Zurich-based design studio founded by Isabel Seiffert and Christoph Miler. Their projects have a strong focus on editorial design, typography, image-making, and storytelling. Next to commissions and collaborations, Offshore Studio investigates critical issues of design, media, and globalisation through self-initiated projects, such as Migrant Journal.
— pp. 54-55, 66-67, 168-171, 192-193

Oliver Meier
www.olli-meier.de

Oliver Meier studied communication design in Münster, Germany, and Edmonton, Canada. Before joining the Monotype team, he worked as a freelancer for a couple of design agencies, such as Meta Design and Stan Hema. He also taught typographic basics at the FHD in Dresden, and his passion lies in design and typography, as well as coding.
— pp. 122-123

Pouya Ahmadi
www.pouyaahmadi.com

Pouya Ahmadi is a Chicago-based typographer and art director. He is also an assistant professor of graphic design at the University of Illinois at Chicago –School of Design– and editorial board member of Neshan magazine, a publication focusing on contemporary graphic design and the visual arts. Pouya's work has been showcased by It's Nice That, aiga Eye on Design; People of Print, Grafik, Etapes, Type Directors Club, Print Magazine, and many others. He holds a master's degree in visual communication from Basel School in Switzerland, and an MFA in Graphic Design from the University of Illinois in Chicago.
— pp. 26-27, 110-111, 184-185, 247-249

Raoul Gottschling
www.raoulgottschling.de

Raoul Gottschling is a German graphic designer based in New York. He graduated from the Düsseldorf University of Applied Sciences in 2017 and was part of büro uebele as well as 2x4 New York before joining Pentagram.
— pp. 244-245

Semiotik
www.semiotikdesign.com

Semiotik's work relies on simplicity, functionality, and effectiveness strongly associated with emotional responsiveness. The studio's design methodology is research-based and aligned with the objectives of each project. This forms the foundation for being truthful to the content, sets the pace for successful outputs, and expands creative opportunities. The team has been fortunate to work with many multinational brands on a wide range of brand development projects, performing in complex environments, and achieving remarkable results. It is happy to work with individuals, small businesses or start-ups to transform new ideas into meaningful propositions. To extend its own thinking,

the team collaborates with other creative specialists to form a proper team for specific projects.
— pp. 38-39, 70-71

Sepus Noordmans
www.sepusnoordmans.com

Sepus Noordmans is a Dutch graphic designer based in The Hague with a strong interest in editorial design, visual identities, web development, and occasional type design. He focuses on design methods that challenge and often cross multiple disciplines and fields, both locally and internationally. He is currently exploring the ongoing relationship between the consumer and advancing technology – which he sometimes reflects in his designs.
— p. 225

Simon Mager
www.simonmager.com

Simon Mager is a German graphic designer based in Lausanne, Switzerland. He graduated from ECAL with a master's degree in art direction, and is a teaching assistant in Master Type Design. Since 2016, he has been working as part of the Omnigroup, operating within the fields of art direction, graphic, and type design.
— pp. 78-80

Studio Feixen
www.studiofeixen.ch

Studio Feixen is an independent design studio based in Lucerne, Switzerland that creates visual concepts that focuses specifically on nothing in particular. Whether it is graphic design, interior design, fashion design, type design or animation – as long as it is challenging – the team is interested. It works internationally with clients like Nike, Google, Hermès, and The New York Times, as well as locally with institutions like the Wanderlust, the Nuits Sonores Festival in France, the Lucerne University of Applied Sciences and Arts, Südpol or the Luzerner Theater.
— p. 131, 206-209, 214-215

Studio Najbrt
www.najbrt.cz

Studio Najbrt is a leading Czech graphic design studio founded in 1994. It creates identities, publications, posters, books, exhibitions, websites and apps for domestic as well as international clients. The studio's longtime collaborations with the Karlovy Vary International Film Festival, the photographer Josef Koudelka, the Ambiente group, the City of Prague and many others established its

bold and playful approach, decorating its imaginary mantelpiece with awards and features in publications from all over the world. "When I think about Studio Najbrt, the first idea that comes to my mind is fun," wrote the design critic, Rick Poynor in 2007, and to this day, no one has objected.
— pp. 86-87, 186-187

The Rodina
www.therodina.com

The Rodina was founded in 2011 by Tereza and Vit Ruller, two Czech-born, Amsterdam-based independent graphic designers. The studio works on commissioned design projects, while experimenting autonomously by inventing ways to preserve and produce experiences, knowledge, and relationships. With interests that lie in the connections between culture, technology, and aesthetics, The Rodina designs events, objects, and tools.
— p. 180, 226-227

Tobias Hönow
tobiashoenow.de

Tobias Hönow holds a B.A. in Visual Communication from the University of Applied Science Düsseldorf. At the moment, he is studying at the Stuttgart State Academy of Art and Design and is a tutor at the Institute for Book Design and Media Development. Since March 2018, he has been working as a Graphic Designer at büro uebele in Stuttgart.
— pp. 244-245

Tor Weibull
www.torweibull.com

Tor Weibull is a Swedish graphic and type designer who earned his bachelor's degree in graphic design at HDK. A semester abroad at ZHDK in Zurich further influenced his practice significantly. As an intern at the Gothenburg-based studio Lundgren+Lindqvist, Tor won Adobe's Nordic Creative Talent Award in 2015. Since graduating, he has been working at Studio Claus Due, and has continued with his own projects and commissions by clients such as Wang & Söderström, and Carl Ander. Tor has recently begun his master's programme in Type Design at ECAL.
— pp. 82-83, 139, 172-173,

VLF Studio
www.vlf-studio.com

VLF Studio is an art direction and design practice in Paris and London, founded by Thomas Cristiani and Antoine Roux.
— pp. 144-145

Ward Heirwegh
www.wardheirwegh.com
sleeperholdpublications.com

Ward Heirwegh graduated in 2007 with a master's degree in graphic design from Luca School of Arts in Ghent, and now runs an independent practice in Antwerp. His projects are situated within the cultural and creative fields through editorial design projects, visual identities, and other commissions for institutions and artists. He teaches graphic design at the St. Lucas School of Arts Antwerp, and has also founded a research-based publication platform called Sleeperhold Publications. In addition to his daily practice, he conducts research into alternative means of distributing information, and is co-founder of a research platform that maps cross-over design practices.
— pp. 40-41, 178-179, 242

Published and distributed by
viction:workshop ltd.

viction:ary™

Unit C, 7th Floor, Seabright Plaza,
9-23 Shell Street, North Point, Hong Kong
URL: www.victionary.com
Email: we@victionary.com

Designed & Edited by TwoPoints.Net

Typefaces in Use:
Caslon 540 LT STD

Second Edition
©2019, 2020 viction:workshop ltd.
The copyright on individual text and design work is held
by the respective designers and contributors.

ISBN 978-988-78501-7-5

The captions and artwork in this book are based on material supplied by the designers whose work is included,
with edits made for clarity. While every effort has been
made to ensure their accuracy, viction:workshop does not
under any circumstances accept any responsibility for any
errors or omissions.

Printed and bound in China

We would like to thank all the designers, studios, and companies who were involved in the production of this book for
their significant contribution to its compilation. We would
also like to express our gratitude to all the producers for
their invaluable opinions and assistance throughout the
entire production process, as well as the many professionals
in the creative industry who have given us precious insights
and comments. Last but not least, to those whose names
are not credited but have made specific inputs in this book,
we thank you for all your efforts and continuous support.